BURT FRANKLIN: RESEARCH & SOURCE WORKS SERIES 581
Essays in Literature & Criticism 95

THE POETS OF TRANSCENDENTALISM

THE POETS OF

TRANSCENDENTALISM

An Anthology

EDITED BY

GEORGE WILLIS COOKE

WITH INTRODUCTORY ESSAY AND
BIOGRAPHICAL NOTES

BURT FRANKLIN
NEW YORK

Published by LENOX HILL Pub. & Dist. Co. (Burt Franklin)
235 East 44th St., New York, N.Y. 10017
Originally Published: 1903
Reprinted: 1970
Printed in the U.S.A.

S.B.N.: 8337-06527
Library of Congress Card Catalog No.: 72-126410
Burt Franklin: Research and Source Works Series 581
Essays in Literature and Criticism 95

Reprinted from the original edition in the University of Texas Library
at Austin.

PREFACE

RECENTLY, in making a somewhat careful and extended study of New England transcendentalism, I was impressed anew by the poetry it produced. I found that much of it had not been republished, and was to be found only in the pages of such periodicals as "The Dial," "The Radical," and "The Journal of Speculative Philosophy." It seemed to me that a representative collection of the poetry influenced by transcendentalism would serve to indicate how largely that movement had affected American literature, and also to make accessible those poems that had been neglected. In making this selection of verse it has not been my aim to choose only what is best, but rather to give specimens of the poetical output of that movement. The selections taken from Emerson, Lowell, and others have been drawn from the pages of the periodicals in which transcendentalism found expression, in order that they may be indicative of the influence coming to these poets from that source. Some of the poems chosen, for that reason, are not to be found in the collected works of these poets. These early, uncollected, or discarded poems are expressive of one or another phase of what transcendentalism was to the youth who accepted it in the flush of its dawn. I have made the collection an inclusive one, without attempting to select from every poet or writer of verses who came into contact with transcendentalism. If the collection has a large number of religious poems it is because this movement was deeply religious in its nature and in its influence.

I have to acknowledge the friendly and generous permission to use their poems given me by Samuel G. Ward, Sydney H. Morse, Thomas W. Higginson, George S. Burleigh, Julia W. Howe, Ednah D. Cheney, John Burroughs, Franklin B. Sanborn, Joel Benton, Augusta C. Bristol, Anna C. Brackett, Francis E. Abbot, John W. Chadwick, William C. Gannett, and Frederick L. Hosmer. I am also indebted to Professor Charles E. Norton for permission to use Lowell's poems, and to Mr. Edward W. Emerson for the use of those of his father. Little, Brown & Company and Lee & Shepard have granted me the use of poems published by them. To McClure, Phillips & Company I am indebted for permission to use one of the poems of John Burroughs; and to the publishers of "Harper's Monthly Magazine" and "The Independent" for the use of poems by Joel Benton.

G. W. C.

CONTENTS

CONTENTS

CONTENTS

CONTENTS

CONTENTS

CONTENTS

CONTENTS

CONTENTS

INTRODUCTION

INTRODUCTION

TRANSCENDENTALISM AND AMERICAN POETRY

THE transcendental movement yet remains the most important influence that has affected American literature. Whatever were its defects — and they were many — it was a creative power, and it gave us our greatest poetry. It is unjust to regard it as an importation from Europe, that might have been excluded by laws against aliens. If the influence of Carlyle, Coleridge, Goethe, and Cousin was considerable, the seed they sowed fell upon good ground here, and speedily germinated. The soil was already prepared for it, and it sprang up as if it were indigenous. Indeed, it is more just to our poets to claim that transcendentalism was native to America than to assert of it that it came from abroad. Its qualities had been in the American mind for generations, perhaps from the first coming of the Puritans. It tempered the teachings of Jonathan Edwards, and it was even in the sermons of Peter Bulkeley, Emerson's earliest American forbear. The "New Divinity" of the eighteenth century was touched by it, and Channing was deeply informed by its life and spirit.

It is not true to what is known as "the transcendental movement," however, to say that it was a thing by itself or a manifestation of a particular type of thought. It was democracy in contact with Puritanism, to define it historically. The free spirit awakened by the establishment of national independence on a basis of liberty and the rights of man, coming into contact with the deep religiousness of Puritanism, and its profound faith in God, gave origin to this movement. It was helped to its formation, but not created, by European philosophy. English and German thinking precipitated the older elements, and gave us the new compound, it may be; but this result was certain to come to pass, even without the foreign aid.

Transcendentalism was a movement of inquiry, revolt against conventionality, and assertion of the worth and dignity of man. It declared that religion is natural to man, that he may trust his own instincts, that individual freedom is essential to a large and wise living, and that spiritual insight is a direct revelation from God. The movement

4

thus developed had a large influence upon Ameri-
can poetry. It may be justly said to have been
the formative power that produced our best liter-
ature. It is impossible to separate it from the
names of Emerson, Lowell, Thoreau, Whittier,
Whitman, and a large company of our lesser poets
and prose writers. That phase of it shown in the
teaching of Wordsworth deeply touched the poetry
of Bryant, and Longfellow was by no means out-
side its movement and its spirit.

This movement influenced not only poetry, but
all forms of writing and thinking. It was not less
creative in the results it produced upon religion
than upon literature. It showed itself in a splen-
did outburst of oratory, that carried its temper and
its convictions widely throughout the country. It
manifested its idealism in numberless movements
for social amelioration and practical reforms. It
was often fanatical, sometimes crude and preten-
tious; and it was even arrogant and domineering.
With all its limitations, however, it was full of life
and inspiration, — noble in motive, wise in con-
ception, and heroic in its loyalty to human wel-
fare. Its tendencies and purposes, especially as
seen in the poetry it produced, may claim from us
a just recognition.

The transcendentalist maintained that the one re-
ality is spirit. Spirit is a unity, but it is also uni-
versal. In the deepest sense spirit is one, though
it may have many manifestations. God is the heart
of all creation, said Emerson; and the heart of
every creature. The one spirit shines in every
human soul, which is nothing apart from that
through which it lives. For the individual soul
the universe has existence only through the Uni-
versal Spirit, which is the essence of the being of
both the individual and the universal.

The transcendentalists often appear to deny the
personality of man, to make him only a manifes-
tation of God. In reality, they laid the greatest
emphasis upon personality, and made of each indi-
vidual man a distinct and unique expression of the
Infinite Spirit. The Over Soul is one in all men,
and yet its manifestation in each is positive and
radical. That which makes man to be man, to
have a character and personality of his own, to be
different from all other creatures and men, is his
immediate connection with the Universal Spirit,
which manifests itself in him in a unique manner.
The Spirit blossoms out in a new form in each in-
dividual man, indeed, as a fresh and distinct crea-
tion. The connection of the individual soul with

the Over Soul is continuous. When the individual so wishes, when he keeps his mind clear and his heart pure, and when his soul is freely open to the life of the Spirit, inspiration will come to him according to his need. He may shut out this light because he refuses to accept it, or because he does not make himself fit for the inflowing of this higher life; but when his soul is open and his life pure he can always have the indwelling of the Spirit.

Individuality was the one essential word and thought of the transcendentalists, and it was what the word connotes in which they believed most strongly. Emerson insisted in his "Fate" that each man must be himself, live his own life, and think his own thought. He would not have the individual dependent upon the activities and interests of other men, as he declares in "Suum Cuique;" but he would have them ever self-centred and independent. Hence it was that he preached self-reliance with an insistence that sometimes makes it seem the only teaching he had to offer. He carried this doctrine to such positive statement as to appear to isolate the individual, and to give him no genuine relations with other men. The atomic social theory was stated in plainest terms by

Christopher P. Cranch in his "Gnosis," when he
declares : —

> We are spirits clad in veils;
>   Man by man was never seen;
> All our deep communing fails
>   To remove the shadowy screen.
>
> Heart to heart was never known;
>   Mind with mind did never meet;
> We are columns left alone
>   Of a temple once complete.
>
> Like the stars that gem the sky,
>   Far apart though seeming near,
> In our light we scattered lie;
>   All is thus but starlight here.

This conception of the individual as an isolated
atom with reference to other individuals, with
which it can have no intimate connection, showed
itself in a frequent insistence upon the right of a
man to act independently of other men. For the
sake of individual perfection, in order that the full
measure of development may be reached, the indi-
vidual ought to ignore social restrictions, and insist
upon his own right to personal expression. This
was emphatically stated by Thoreau in his " Con-
science," wherein he said, —

I love a soul not all of wood,
Predestinated to be good,
But true to the backbone
Unto itself alone,
And false to none.

The last clause appears to qualify the emphatic individualism of this position, and to give recognition to social obligations; but the insistence upon the right to personal development and assertion is so strong that all else disappears in comparison. To be one's self is made the absolute controlling interest and purpose of life.

This metaphysical atomism is almost inevitable, in view of the transcendentalist's doctrine of continuous inspiration to the soul that is fit therefor. When the source of truth is not human, the result of experience and of social growth, but of direct contact of the individual soul with the Over Soul, it follows that the individual seeks in himself truth and guidance. What other men think does not concern him. To the universal experiences of the race he is indifferent. Racial inspiration he regards as impossible, and for the genius of a people he has no concern. But let us not overlook the actual faith of the transcendentalist. In reality, Emerson's "self-reliance" is God-reliance. It is trust in the inward truth that comes to the soul from its immediate contact with the Over Soul. "The Problem" is a statement of this doctrine of direct personal inspiration, which is the source, according to Emerson, of all genius as manifested in art, literature, or religion.

> The *passive* Master lent his hand
> To the vast Soul that o'er him planned.

For the genius this is true, in the thought of the transcendentalist; and for the common man not less. Whatever of life and capacity is in either is the result of his inspiration received from the Over Soul. In himself he can do nothing. It is the Over Soul that does all things through him, using his powers for other ends than his own. The Voice is always speaking, says Lowell in "Bibliolatres," and whoever will listen intently enough, in the right way, will hear its word of life. Not only are the Bibles of the world its utterances, but in all times and in all men it speaks its divine word. Thoreau held that the poet cannot sing truly without this inward contact with the Over Soul. It brings him gift of song, and it gives him eternal things to sing.

> I hear beyond the range of sound,
> I see beyond the range of sight.

Lowell was deeply influenced in his early life by this conception of the mission of the poet. He seems to have believed that there can be no true poetry written without the direct aid of the Over Soul. His biographer says of the period when he was writing his " Conversations on Some of the Old Poets," that " he more than once hinted darkly that he was not writing the book, but was the spokesman for sages and poets who used him as their means of communication." That he was the spokesman of the Over Soul was Lowell's strong belief at this period, for we find him writing in a letter, " I have always been a very Quaker in following the Light, and writing only when the Spirit moved." In September, 1842, he described a conversation in which this feeling of divine contact was almost overpowering. "I had a revelation last Friday evening. As I was speaking the whole system rose up before me like a vague Destiny looming from the abyss. I never before so clearly felt the spirit of God in me and around me. The whole room seemed to me full of God. The air seemed to wave to and fro with the presence of Something, I knew not what. I spoke with the calmness and clearness of a prophet."

Even more distinctly was this conception of im-

mediate revelation that of Jones Very, who main-
tained that he was only the spokesman of the
higher powers. He claimed that his sonnets on
religious subjects contained a message "given
him" by the Spirit. In sending to Emerson the
manuscript of his essays and poems, he wrote: "I
am glad at last to transmit what has been *told me*
of Shakespeare. You hear not mine own words,
but the teachings of the Holy Ghost." What he
wrote, was his belief, "came" to him, and was not
the product of his own mind. The Voice uttered
itself through him, and he was but the medium of
its expression. He said of what he had written:
"I value these verses, not because they are *mine*,
but because they are *not*." This conception of
immediate contact with the Over Soul was widely
accepted by the transcendentalists, and it had a
large influence upon their poetry and its literary
content.

They also held that this inward conception of
life is one of large hope to the toiler, and of pa-
tience to those who cannot labor. It is the source
of life, the joy of living, in every one who truly
lives. In so far as he dwells in the Over Soul
does he realize in himself the meaning and the worth
of life. And it was this conception of man's rela-

tions to the Over Soul that made Emerson say, that all we can learn by travel is to be known at home. Europe can give us nothing of life that is unknown in Concord, simply because the deep experiences of life, those that enrich mind and heart, are the gift of the Spirit. They are not the result of contact with other men, the study of the social products of ages of human endeavor in the past, but of immediate touch with the informing spirit of life. It is not man who is our teacher, but the Over Soul. We need not have the highest truths mediated to us through art, literature, philosophy; but the spirit informs us out of its own rich and abundant life. The Over Soul can reach us at home as readily, and even with greater certainty, than in foreign lands. What the Soul reveals cannot be added to by going up and down in the world. It is even true that the outward shows hinder us from the true things of the inward life. In quietness and humbleness of spirit we learn what cannot be revealed amidst the noises and distractions of the world. It is this conception of the worth of inward human experiences that made Ellery Channing say, in his " Confessio Amantis," that he knew all that even the greatest men have gained from life.

Dion or Cæsar drained no more,
Not Solon, nor a Plato's lore ;
So much had they the power to do,
So much hadst thou, and equals too.

It is this conception of the relations of the poet to the Over Soul that makes him a seer and a prophet. This oracular mood is in much of Emerson's writing, and it is in that of many of the other transcendentalist writers. It gives peculiarity to the works of Thoreau, Alcott, Margaret Fuller, and many others. They are speaking with the authority of a higher life than their own. This gives them an attitude of immense egotism on occasion. If the individuality is not too insistent, it gives force, dignity, power, to the words they employ ; and a high ethical quality. Emerson often seems to speak in tones of command, to utter eternal words. We tire of this quality when it is too persistent, however, for the lofty height, the demand for what we have not attained, repels us, and makes rebellion necessary. We joy in it at times, but we cannot always breathe the mountain air. And yet, Emerson is so much the rebel against all that is presumptuous, dogmatic, opinionated, that he takes sides himself against whatever is authoritative in his own words. He is a seer, but not

14

one who commands the loyalty of other men to his own beliefs.

Inwardness is a frequent note of the transcendental poet. He loves nature, but he lives in his own thoughts. The outward as outward does not appeal to him. It is the indwelling of the Universal Spirit that sustains him; and he turns from the objective world, especially from social forms and religious conventionalisms, to find in himself, as the dwelling-place of the Spirit, that which is beautiful and inspiring. Lowell could not find true nobleness in the men and women around him; but he was bade

> Look inward through the depths of thine own soul,

and then he found it, even in others. Very saw on earth another light than that his eye revealed, which

> Came forth as from my soul within
> And from a higher sky;

and it is this inward light to which he goes for guidance.

> It shone from God within.

Another poet said it is not in nature we are to find God, but the inner eye reveals him to us.

15

Nature all concealing,
Dim her outer light,
Finite forms revealing,
Not the infinite.

The Over Soul is revealed in the outward world, but rather as a foil than as an expression of its highest life. When man would know the largest measure of being, he must turn away from nature, and seek it in his own soul. When he turns inward, and puts away selfishness and all regard for material things, humbly submits himself to the guidance of the Spirit, he will then find the divine life he seeks. Many of our poets agree with Wordsworth in the conviction that the world is too much with us, and they turned away from it to find in the soul the light that never was on sea or land. Nature is of value to man because it reflects himself to himself, and enables him to look at his own life as it is mirrored back to him from the physical world. It is capable of interpreting man to himself because it is an expression of the Over Soul in another kind. It has the same life that is in man, but without his individuality and liberty. Its permanence, its want of emotion, its passive acceptance of the Spirit that in it finds manifestation, shows man the need he has for integrity of soul and imperturbability of spirit.

> All around himself he lies,

said Alcott of man, for nature is the reflection of man, and man the measure of nature.

> Nature's the eyeball of the Mind,

said Alcott again. It is this unity of man and nature, the marvelous way in which they reflect and interpret each other, that gives origin to the doctrine of correspondences, which was accepted in greater or less degree by all the transcendental poets. This theory was fully stated by Cranch in his declaration:

> All things in Nature are beautiful types to the Soul that will read them ;
> Nothing exists upon earth but for unspeakable ends.
> Every object that speaks to the senses was meant for the spirit ;
> Nature is but a scroll, God's handwriting thereon.

According to this theory there is between the material and the spiritual worlds an intimate relation ; and the spiritual is interpreted to man by means of the material, which is its image or eidolon. It is as such an expression of the Over Soul that nature is of chief interest to our poets. They may love it for its beauty, but it is of greater worth to them as a manifestation of the spirit that shines through it. Nature is a perfect image of God in its own kind, without freedom of will or ethical liberty. Reason is absent from it, and it is also without the defect of vice, crime, and sin. It is not God, but God is reflected in it as in a mirror. We catch glimpses of his image therein, and they charm and console us. There in some measure is his law written, and there we come into intimate sympathy with him and his abundant life.

The transcendentalist's conception of the relations of mind and body, and his belief not only that mind is fundamental but that it is the only reality, led him to a degree of asceticism. He looked upon the body as the servant of the mind, and therefore he would keep it in strictest subjection. This subordination of the physical part of man led to a strict regimen, to the practice of temperance, and even to abstemiousness. The mind ought to dominate the body, and if it is true to itself the body will know no ill. It is sin of mind that makes disease of body, according to the transcendentalist. When the mind dwells in the body with poise and integrity, the body will be sound and whole. This doctrine is well stated by Very :

Not from the earth, or skies,
　Or seasons as they roll,
Come health and vigor to the frame,
　But from the living soul.

Is this alive to God,
　And not the slave to sin?
Then will the body, too, receive
　Health from the soul within.

For He who formed our frame
　Made man a perfect whole,
And made the body's health depend
　Upon the living soul.

According to Emerson the soul is the man, and it uses the functions of the body for its purposes. It is "the background of our being," the light that shines through the bodily form. When the mind is sound the body is whole, and all defect of body is first of all defect of mind. The remedy for ills of the physical nature is the setting the mind in order and the living in harmony with its laws.

The transcendentalist is always an optimist. Because he believes in the Over Soul he is confident that evil is but temporary, and that it will pass away as the spirit is more perfectly revealed in the evolution of man. While he sometimes accepts the "lapse" philosophy, as did Alcott, and maintains that man has through self-will fallen from a more perfect state, he always believes in the gradual recovery of the higher nature, or the development of man until he shall fully attain to the things of the spirit and live a noble life. He believes that the future is better than the past, that Paradise is before and not behind. This belief is definitely stated by Miss Clapp: —

> Eden with its angels bold,
> Love and flowers and coolest sea,
> Is not ancient story told,
> But a glowing prophecy.

It was this confidence in the development of man that made one of these poets sing of a present heaven, and another of the workers as coming surely to their own, the best the world contains. Heaven is of the present as well as of the future, and begins here to show its quality and its worth.

The transcendentalist was confident of immortality. He not only had faith that man will live hereafter, but he was also possessed of knowledge, as he thought. " I know I am immortal," was his confident assertion. His desire became, as it were, an intuition, and that he held was enough to assure him of the future.

I am immortal ! I know it ! I feel it !

was the strong declaration of Margaret Fuller.

Chance cannot touch me ! Time cannot hush me !
    Fear, Hope, and Longing, at strife,
Sink as I rise, on, on, upward forever,
Gathering strength, gaining breath, — naught can sever
    Me from the spirit of Life !

It was confident faith in Spirit that gave such as-
surance of futurity. It made Ellery Channing
sing in that noble line — one of the finest in the
language —

If my bark sink, 't is to another sea,

with a profound conviction based on the deepest
faith. But Emerson struck another note on this
subject, one less assertive, even if as trustful. As
was characteristic of the man, he was reticent of
dogmatic claims, and trusted the future without
presumptive assertion. He once declared : " We
may hope for a future life, that will enable us to
see things once, and then to pass on to something
new." Such a statement, if less confident, is more
rational.

A strong ethical tendency manifests itself in
many of the transcendental poets, as in Sill's
" Life," Hooper's " True Nobleness," and Howe's

"Warning." Their optimism did not relax the moral purpose, but made it even more vigorous and insistent. There was something heroic in their teaching, and they braced the soul for duty, and the mind to accept the whole of the truth. Emerson is one of the most ethical of teachers, and always preaches a gospel of courage, strenuous fidelity, and insistent loyalty. He ethically invigorates all who come into real contact with him, and helps them to face life without flinching and with joyous confidence.

This courage grows out of a profound trust in the Over Soul. The heart of the world is sound, and its will can be accepted without fear. Our poets therefore joyfully accept the ways of the Over Soul. They wait its manifestations with hope, and do not seek to make their own purposes overtop it. The universe is inherently good, and there is no call to despair for those who see it as it is. Tranquillity, peace of soul, moderation in desire, are virtues cultivated by those who put their trust in the ways of the Over Soul. There is no need to run up and down the world for beauty, or help, or truth, for all these the Spirit brings to those who need them.

> I stay my haste, I make delays,
>   For what avails this eager pace?
> I stand amid the eternal ways,
>   And what is mine shall know my face.

When Burroughs sings in this fashion he shows himself a true transcendentalist, for that is the attitude and temper of this faith. It does not question the ways of the Over Soul, which is one with its own highest good. It has no creed, no dogma, no ritual, no infallible scripture; but the soul trusts that what is true and right and just will assert itself, and will make itself clearly known. Therefore, it does not combat evil, but seeks the good. It is so trustful of the Over Soul that it will not strive or complain, but hopefully accepts what the Spirit gives.

The chief defect of the poetry of the transcendentalists is that it is too philosophical. Its largest intent is ethical or religious, and not artistic. Beauty is not its chief inspiration, but thought. It is not written to please, but to convince. It contains a gospel, and not an appeal to emotion and imagination. That this defect always presents itself it would not be just to say, and yet it is too often present. These poets are more concerned as to what they say than as to how they say it. They are not singers, but teachers. The problems of life much concern them, and how to reform the world is to them of great importance. The charm of their poetry is in the beauty of the thought, and not in the delight of the song they sing. The form is often rugged, the verse is halting and defective. Their metres stumble, and their rhymes are not correct. They are too metaphysical, subtle, and complicated in their thought to sing themselves clearly and strongly out into beautiful words. Their thought is involved, and often obscure. They are so charmed with what they have to say, and it is of such a complex and subjective nature, that they cannot find simple and direct speech for its utterance. Hence the halting nature of their verse, its crippled metres, and its defective rhymes. Too often in their verse they are not poets, but philosophers.

These poets do not sing for the joy of the singing; and yet it was their idealism, the fact that they were enamored of beautiful thoughts, that made them use the verse form instead of prose. Poetry was to all of them the occasional rather than the chief medium of expression. With the exception of Lowell, they were not poets by profession, and even with him prose was used oftener than verse.

INTRODUCTION

Although Emerson early declared that his calling was that of a poet, yet he gave to the lecture and the essay the preference. With Thoreau, Margaret Fuller, Higginson, and Wasson, as well as others, poetry was occasional or incidental. To a larger number poetry was an accident, and they wrote one or two or a half dozen poems only. There was something in transcendentalism that made them poets in youth or at rare moments; but they were grave theologians or philosophers for the rest of their lives. They were so stirred by the joy of life or the beauties of nature that prose ceased to be a fit medium for their thoughts. When verse thus became necessary to them they used it with a considerable degree of success, and these rare utterances are far above the level of occasional verse, whatever their defects.

If poetry is an interpretation of life, the transcendental poets deserve a large recognition. If their metaphysics repels us, and their subjectiveness is too subtle and insistent, they saw life largely and sanely. We can forgive their defective rhymes in view of their noble optimism and their heroic ethical temper. With them the man is more than the verse, and the manhood shines through the stumbling metres. If there is too much philosophy in their poetry, the teaching is sound and it is sincere. It was indeed a gospel they gave to those who need it.

Transcendentalism no longer holds the place it once occupied. It is not now the inspirer of poets or the chief influence in our literature. While idealism is more firmly established and more widely accepted than ever, transcendentalism has lost its intellectual supremacy. Its defects are not far to seek, and its excesses have discredited much that it taught. That mind is all, and that the Over Soul speaks only to the individual mind, are assertions that are widely criticised at the present time. The " intuitions " of the transcendentalist find a saner interpretation in the subtle laws of heredity than in the explanation he gave them. Individualism gives way to a recognition of social forces. The atomic theory of the soul does not justify itself in view of our present knowledge of social interaction. But not all the transcendentalists were contented with the theory that the individual is an isolated expression of the Over Soul. The larger view was justly stated by George Ripley and William Henry Channing, who vigorously protested against Emerson's individualism and what it implied. Self-reliance has its worth, but no man can isolate himself from his kind, even in the name of the Over Soul. A " rather mountainous Me," as was said of Margaret Fuller's self-assertion, shows itself in too many who accept the doctrine of self-reliance. They ignore the heredity that has determined their capacities, the social forces that have created their opportunities, and the spiritual ideals of the race that have given them their motives and their vision.

We may give to transcendentalism a generous recognition for what it was to the men and women who accepted it; but we must see in it a passing phase of American thought. It may be that there are a larger number of persons who accept this faith to-day than in the prime of the movement as it affected American literature; but it is now an echo. To no great men is it inspiration, and it develops no creative literary movement. The charm of it has passed away as a vital force. It is a beautiful memory that is precious and glorious, and that still charms and delights us.

That it will revive again we may be convinced. It represents one of the persistent types of human thought. To some minds it is always true, because there are always individuals who see the world in this manner. It rarely happens, however, that this form of thought is widely enough accepted to constitute a "movement" or to create a literature. When this occurs the legacy is precious, and we may well cherish it with care and with joy. We can delight in what it is and in what it accomplishes without accepting its philosophy. No one of to-day can put himself back into the full spirit of that movement and realize the complete measure of it; but to appreciate it, to give it large recognition and just credit for what it was, that is not essential. Every age has its own type and quality, and reproduces none that has gone before it; but it ought to be able to see largely and sympathetically what other men and other ages have accomplished. If their time is not our time, and their thought not our thought, we have a large duty that requires us to give them wise recognition and to credit them with the great debt we owe them. Thus it is we may applaud the transcendentalists, praise unstintedly their work, take large delight in what they accomplished for American literature, without accepting their ethical theories or their religious philosophy. They were deeply religious men, but we need a more scientific word than was theirs. That they were seers, we admit; but we cannot sit with them in the prophet's garb. And yet, we praise them, for we are glad in their work. What they wrought of beauty, art, philosophy, religion, is ours ; and we have no wish to turn aside from the inheritance. We take it as a goodly part of what the past has placed in store for us.

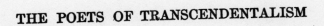

THE POETS OF TRANSCENDENTALISM

Ralph Waldo Emerson

EACH AND ALL

LITTLE thinks, in the field, yon red-cloaked clown,
Of thee from the hill-top looking down;
The heifer that lows in the upland farm,
Far-heard, lows not thine ear to charm;
The sexton, tolling his bell at noon,
Deems not that great Napoleon
Stops his horse and lists with delight,
Whilst his files sweep round yon Alpine height;
Nor knowest thou what argument
Thy life to thy neighbor's creed has lent.
All are needed by each one;
Nothing is fair or good alone.
I thought the sparrow's note from heaven,
Singing at dawn on the alder bough;
I brought him home, in his nest, at even;
He sings the song, but it cheers not now,
For I did not bring home the river and sky; —
He sang to my ear, — they sang to my eye.
The delicate shells lay on the shore;
The bubbles of the latest wave
Fresh pearls to their enamel gave,

And the bellowing of the savage sea
Greeted their safe escape to me.
I wiped away the weeds and foam,
I fetched my sea-born treasures home;
But the poor, unsightly, noisome things
Had left their beauty on the shore
With the sun and the sand and the wild uproar.
The lover watched his graceful maid,
As mid the virgin train she strayed,
Nor knew her beauty's best attire
Was woven still by the snow-white choir.
At last she came to his hermitage,
Like the bird from the woodlands to the cage; —
The gay enchantment was undone,
A gentle wife, but fairy none.
Then I said, " I covet truth;
Beauty is unripe childhood's cheat;
I leave it behind with the games of youth: " —
As I spoke, beneath my feet
The ground-pine curled its pretty wreath,
Running over the club-moss burrs;
I inhaled the violet's breath;
Around me stood the oaks and firs;
Pine-cones and acorns lay on the ground;
Over me soared the eternal sky,
Full of light and of deity;

THE RHODORA

Again I saw, again I heard,
The rolling river, the morning bird; —
Beauty through my senses stole;
I yielded myself to the perfect whole.

THE RHODORA:

ON BEING ASKED, WHENCE IS THE FLOWER?

In May, when sea-winds pierced our solitudes,
I found the fresh Rhodora in the woods,
Spreading its leafless blooms in a damp nook,
To please the desert and the sluggish brook.
The purple petals, fallen in the pool,
Made the black water with their beauty gay;
Here might the red-bird come his plumes to cool,
And court the flower that cheapens his array.
Rhodora! if the sages ask thee why
This charm is wasted on the earth and sky,
Tell them, dear, that if eyes were made for seeing,
Then Beauty is its own excuse for being:
Why thou wert there, O rival of the rose!
I never thought to ask, I never knew:
But in my simple ignorance, suppose
The self-same Power that brought me there brought
    you.

THE PROBLEM

I LIKE a church ; I like a cowl ;
I love a prophet of the soul ;
And on my heart monastic aisles
Fall like sweet strains, or pensive smiles :
Yet not for all his faith can see
Would I that cowlèd churchman be.

Why should the vest on him allure,
Which I could not on me endure ?

Not from a vain or shallow thought
His awful Jove young Phidias brought ;
Never from lips of cunning fell
The thrilling Delphic oracle ;
Out from the heart of nature rolled
The burdens of the Bible old ;
The litanies of nations came,
Like the volcano's tongue of flame,
Up from the burning core below, —
The canticles of love and woe :
The hand that rounded Peter's dome
And groined the aisles of Christian Rome

Wrought in a sad sincerity ;
Himself from God he could not free ;
He builded better than he knew ; —
The conscious stone to beauty grew.

Know'st thou what wove yon woodbird's nest
Of leaves, and feathers from her breast ?
Or how the fish outbuilt her shell,
Painting with morn each annual cell ?
Or how the sacred pine-tree adds
To her old leaves new myriads ?
Such and so grew these holy piles,
Whilst love and terror laid the tiles.
Earth proudly wears the Parthenon
As the best gem upon her zone,
And Morning opes with haste her lids
To gaze upon the Pyramids ;
O'er England's abbeys bends the sky,
As on its friends, with kindred eye ;
For out of Thought's interior sphere
These wonders rose to upper air ;
And Nature gladly gave them place,
Adopted them into her race,
And granted them an equal date
With Andes and with Ararat.

These temples grew as grows the grass;
Art might obey, but not surpass.
The passive Master lent his hand
To the vast soul that o'er him planned;
And the same power that reared the shrine
Bestrode the tribes that knelt within.
Ever the fiery Pentecost
Girds with one flame the countless host,
Trances the heart through chanting choirs,
And through the priest the mind inspires.
The word unto the prophet spoken
Was writ on tables yet unbroken;
The word by seers or sibyls told,
In groves of oak, or fanes of gold,
Still floats upon the morning wind,
Still whispers to the willing mind.
One accent of the Holy Ghost
The heedless world hath never lost.
I know what say the fathers wise, —
The Book itself before me lies,
Old Chrysostom, best Augustine,
And he who blent both in his line,
The younger Golden Lips or mines,
Taylor, the Shakespeare of divines.
His words are music in my ear,
I see his cowlèd portrait dear;

And yet, for all his faith could see,
I would not the good bishop be.

THE ETERNAL PAN

ALL the forms are fugitive,
But the substances survive.
Ever fresh the broad creation,
A divine improvisation,
From the heart of God proceeds,
A single will, a million deeds.
Once slept the world an egg of stone,
And pulse, and sound, and light was none;
And God said, "Throb!" and there was motion
And the vast mass became vast ocean.
Onward and on, the eternal Pan,
Who layeth the world's incessant plan,
Halteth never in one shape,
But forever doth escape,
Like wave or flame, into new forms
Of gem, and air, of plants, and worms.
I, that to-day am a pine,
Yesterday was a bundle of grass.
He is free and libertine,
Pouring of his power the wine

To every age, to every race ;
Unto every race and age
He emptieth the beverage ;
Unto each and unto all,
Maker and original.
The world is the ring of his spells,
And the play of his miracles.
As he giveth to all to drink,
Thus or thus they are and think.
With one drop sheds form and feature ;
With the next a special nature ;
The third adds heat's indulgent spark ;
The fourth gives light which eats the dark ;
Into the fifth himself he flings,
And conscious Law is King of kings.
As the bee through the garden ranges,
From world to world the godhead changes ;
As the sheep go feeding in the waste,
From form to form He maketh haste ;
This vault which glows immense with light
Is the inn where he lodges for a night.
What recks such Traveller if the bowers
Which bloom and fade like meadow flowers
A bunch of fragrant lilies be,
Or the stars of eternity ?
Alike to him the better, the worse, —

The glowing angel, the outcast corse.
Thou metest him by centuries,
And lo! he passes like the breeze;
Thou seek'st in glade and galaxy,
He hides in pure transparency;
Thou askest in fountains and in fires,
He is the essence that inquires.
He is the axis of the star;
He is the sparkle of the spar;
He is the heart of every creature;
He is the meaning of each feature;
And his mind is the sky,
Than all it holds more deep, more high.

FATE

THAT you are fair or wise is vain,
Or strong, or rich, or generous;
You must have also the untaught strain
That sheds beauty on the rose.
There is a melody born of melody
Which melts the world into a sea.
Toil could never compass it,
Art its height could never hit,
It came never out of wit;

41

But a music music-born
Well may Jove and Juno scorn.
Thy beauty, if it lack the fire
Which drives me mad with sweet desire,
What boots it?   What the soldier's mail,
Unless he conquer and prevail?
What all the goods thy pride which lift,
If thou pine for another's gift?
Alas! that one is born in blight,
Victim of perpetual slight:
When thou lookest on his face,
Thy heart saith, Brother! go thy ways!
None shall ask thee what thou doest,
Or care a rush for what thou knowest,
Or listen when thou repliest,
Or remember where thou liest,
Or how thy supper is sodden, —
And another is born
To make the sun forgotten.
Surely he carries a talisman
Under his tongue,
Broad are his shoulders, and strong,
And his eye is scornful,
Threatening and young.
I hold it of little matter,
Whether your jewel be of pure water,

A rose diamond or a white,
But whether it dazzle me with light.
I care not how you are drest,
In the coarsest or in the best,
Nor whether your name is base or brave,
Nor for the fashion of your behavior,
But whether you charm me,
Bid my bread feed and my fire warm me,
And dress up nature in your favor.
One thing is forever good, —
That one thing is Success,
Dear to the Eumenides,
And to all the heavenly brood.
Who bides at home, nor looks abroad,
He carries the eagles — he masters the sword.

James Russell Lowell

THE FRANKNESS OF NATURE

WHEN in a book I find a pleasant thought
Which some small flower in the woods to me
Had told, as if in straitest secrecy,
That I might speak it in sweet verses wrought,
With what best feelings is such meeting fraught!
It shows how nature's life will never be
Shut up from speaking out full clear and free
Her wonders to the soul that will be taught.
And what though I have but this single chance
Of saying that which every gentle soul
Shall answer with a glad, uplifting glance?
Nature is frank to him whose spirit whole
Doth love Truth more than praise, and in good
      time,
My flower will tell me sweeter things to rhyme.

THE POET'S OBEDIENCE

ONLY as thou herein canst not see me,
Only as thou the same low voice canst hear

Which is the morning song of every sphere
And which thou erewhile heardst beside the sea
Or in the still night flowing solemnly,
Only so love this rhyme and so revere;
All else cast from thee, haply with a tear
For one who, rightly taught, yet would not be
A voice obedient; some things I have seen
With a clear eye, and otherwhile the earth
With a most sad eclipse hath come between
That sunlight which is mine by right of birth
And what I know with grief I ought to have
      been, —
Yet is short-coming even something worth.

TO IRENE ON HER BIRTHDAY

MAIDEN, when such a soul as thine is born,
The morning stars their ancient music make
And joyful once again their song awake,
Long silent now with melancholy scorn;
And thou, not mindless of so blest a morn,
By no least deed its harmony shall break,
And shalt to that high clime thy footsteps take
Through life's most darksome passes unfor-
      lorn;

Therefore from thy pure faith thou shalt not
  fall,
Therefore shalt thou be ever fair and free
And in thine every motion musical
As summer air, majestic as the sea,
A mystery to those who creep and crawl
Through Time and part it from Eternity.

WISDOM OF THE ETERNAL ONE

THEREFORE think not the Past is wise alone,
For Yesterday knows nothing of the Best,
And thou shalt love it only as the nest
Whence glory-wingèd things to Heaven have flown :
To the great Soul alone are all things known ;
Present and future are to her as past,
While she in glorious madness doth forecast
That perfect bud, which seems a flower full-blown
To each new Prophet, and yet always opes
Fuller and fuller with each day and hour,
Heartening the soul with odor of fresh hopes,
And longings high, and gushings of wide power,
Yet never is or shall be fully blown
Save in the forethought of the Eternal One.

WINTER

THE bird sings not in winter-time,
  Nor doth the happy murmur of the bees
Swarm round us from the chill, unleavèd lime,
And shall ye hear the poet o' sunny rhyme,
  Mid souls more bleak and bare than winter
      trees?

As a lone singing bird that far away,
  Hath follow'd north the fickle smiles of spring,
Is ambush'd by a sudden bitter day,
And sits forlorn upon a leafless spray,
  Hiding his head beneath his numbèd wing,

So is the poet, if he chance to fall
  'Mong hearts by whom he is not understood,
Dull hearts, whose throbbing grows not musical,
Although their strings are blown upon by all
  The sweetest breezes of the true and good.

His spirit pineth orphan'd of that home
  Wherein was nursed its wondrous infancy,
And whence sometimes 'neath night's all-quiet
      dome,

47

Swiftly a wingèd memory will come,
  And prophesy of glory yet to be.

Then knows he that he hath not been exiled
  From those wide walls his own by right of birth;
But hath been sent, a well-belovèd child,
A chosen one on whom his father smiled,
  And blest, to be his messenger on Earth.

Then doth his brow with its right glory shine,
  And stretching forth his strong, undaunted wings,
He soareth to an atmosphere divine,
Whence he can see afar that clime benign,
  His fatherland, whose mystic song he sings.

So in his eyes there doth such blessings grow,
  That all those faces erst so hard and dull,
With a sweet warmth of brotherhood do glow,
As he had seen them glisten long ago,
  In that old home so free and beautiful.

LOVE REFLECTED IN NATURE

Our love is not a fading earthly flower;
Its wingèd seed dropped down from Paradise,

THE STREET

And nursed by day and night, by sun and shower,
Doth momently to fresher beauty rise;
To us the leafless autumn is not bare,
Nor winter's rattling boughs lack lusty green,
Our summer hearts make summer's fulness where
No leaf or bud or blossom may be seen:
For nature's life in lover's deep life doth lie,
Love — whose forgetfulness is beauty's death,
Whose mystic key these cells of thou and I
Into the infinite freedom openeth,
And makes the body's dark and narrow grate
The wide-flung leaves of heaven's palace-gate.

THE STREET

THEY pass by me like shadows, crowds on crowds,
Dim ghosts of men, that hover to and fro,
Hugging their bodies round them like thin shrouds
Wherein their souls were buried long ago;
They trampled on their faith and youth and love —
They cast their hope of human kind away —
With Heaven's clear messages they madly strove
And conquered, — and their spirits turned to clay;
Lo! how they wander round the world, their
    grave,

49

Whose ever-gaping maw by such is fed,
Gibbering at living men, and idly rave
" We only truly live, but ye are dead," —
Alas, poor fools! the anointed eye may trace
A dead soul's epitaph in every face.

BIBLIOLATRES

GOD is not dumb, that he should speak no more;
If thou hast wanderings in the wilderness
And find'st not Sinai, 't is thy soul is poor;
There towers the mountain of the Voice no
    less,
Which whoso seeks shall find, but he who bends,
Intent on manna still and mortal ends,
Sees it not, neither hears its thundered lore.

Slowly the Bible of the race is writ,
And not on paper leaves nor leaves of stone;
Each age, each kindred, adds a verse to it,
Texts of despair or hope, of joy or moan.
While swings the sea, while mists the mountains
        shroud,
While thunder's surges burst on cliffs of cloud,
Still at the prophets' feet the nation sit.

DIVINE TEACHERS

God sends his teachers unto every age,
To every clime and every race of men,
With revelations fitted to their growth
And shape of mind, nor gives the realm of Truth
Into the selfish rule of one sole race:
Therefore each form of worship that hath swayed
The life of man, and given it to grasp
The master-key of knowledge, reverence,
Infolds some germs of goodness and of right;
Else never had the eager soul, which loathes
The slothful down of pampered ignorance,
Found in it even a moment's fitful rest.

There is an instinct in the human heart
Which makes that all the fables it hath coined,
To justify the reign of its belief
And strengthen it by beauty's right divine,
Veil in their inner cells a mystic gift,
Which, like the hazel twig, in faithful hands,
Points surely to the hidden springs of truth.
For, as in nature naught is made in vain,
But all things have within their hull of use
A wisdom and a meaning which may speak

Of spiritual secrets to the ear
Of spirit; so, in whatsoe'er the heart
Hath fashioned for a solace to itself,
To make its inspiration suit its creed,
And from the niggard hands of falsehood wring
Its needful food of truth, there ever is
A sympathy with Nature, which reveals,
Not less than her own works, pure gleams of light
And earnest parables of inward lore.

TRUE NOBLENESS

" For this true nobleness I seek in vain,
In woman and in man I find it not;
I almost weary of my earthly lot,
My life-springs are dried up with burning pain."
Thou find'st it not?   I pray thee look again,
Look inward through the depths of thine own soul.
How is it with thee?   Art thou sound and whole?
Doth narrow search show thee no earthly stain?
Be noble! and the nobleness that lies
In other men, sleeping, but never dead,
Will rise in majesty to meet thine own;
Then wilt thou see it gleam in many eyes,
Then will pure light around thy path be shed,
And thou wilt nevermore be sad and lone.

Amos Bronson Alcott

MAN

HE omnipresent is,
All round himself he lies,
Osiris spread abroad,
Upstaring in all eyes :
Nature has globèd thought,
Without him she were not,
Cosmos from Chaos were not spoken,
And God bereft of visible token.

APPROACHING GOD

WHEN thou approachest to the One,
Self from thyself thou first must free,
Thy cloak duplicity cast clean aside,
And in thy Being's being be.

MATTER

OUT of the chaos dawns in sight
The globe's full form in orbèd light ;

Beam kindles beam, kind mirrors kind,
Nature's the eyeball of the Mind;
The fleeting pageant tells for nought
Till shaped in Mind's creative thought.

FRIENDSHIP

NOR elsewise man shall fellow meet,
In public place, in converse sweet,
In holy aisles, at market gate,
In learning's halls, or courts of state,
Nor persons properly shall find,
Save in the commonwealth of Mind;
Fair forms herein their souls intrude,
Peopling what else were solitude.

EXCELLENCE

WHERE is that good, which wise men please to
    call
The chiefest?   Doth any such befall
Within man's reach? or is there such a good at
    all?

If such there be, it neither must expire
Nor change; than which there can be nothing
      higher:
Such good must be the utter point of man's desire.

It is the mark to which all hearts must tend;
Can be desired for no other end
Than for itself, on which all other goods depend.

What may this excellence be?   Doth it subsist
A real essence clouded in the mist
Of curious art, or clear to every eye that list?

Or is 't a tart idea, to procure
An edge, and keep the practice soul in ure
Like that dear chymic dust, or puzzling quadrature?

Where shall I seek this good? where shall I find
This cath'lic pleasure, whose extremes may bind
My thoughts, and fill the gulf of my insatiate
      mind?

Lies it in treasure? in full heaps untold?
Doth gouty Mammon's griping hand infold
This secret saint in secret shrines of sov'reign gold?

No, no, she lies not there ; wealth often sours
In keeping ; makes us hers, in seeming ours ;
She slides from Heaven indeed, but not in Danae's
    showers.

Lives she in honor ?   No.   The royal crown
Builds up a creature, and then batters down :
Kings raise thee with a smile and raze thee with
    a frown.

In pleasure ?   No.   Pleasure begins in rage ;
Acts the fool's part on earth's uncertain stage :
Begins the play in youth, and epilogues in age.

These, these are bastard goods ; the best of these
Torment the soul with pleasing it ; and please,
Like waters gulp'd in fevers, with deceitful ease.

Earth's flatt'ring dainties are but sweet distresses,
Mole-hills perform the mountains she professes,
Alas ! can earth confer more good than earth pos-
    sesses ?

Mount, mount, my soul, and let my thoughts cashier
Earth's vain delights, and make thy full career
At Heaven's eternal joys : stop, stop, thy courser
    there.

There shall thy soul possess uncareful treasure:
There shalt thou swim in never-fading pleasure,
And blaze in honor far above the frowns of Cæsar.

Lord, if my hope dare let her anchor fall,
On thee, the chiefest good, no need to call
For earth's inferior trash; thou, thou art All in All.

THE SEER'S RATIONS

TAKES sunbeams, spring waters,
Earth's juices, meads' creams,
Bathes in floods of sweet ethers,
Comes baptized from the streams;
Guest of Him, the sweet-lipp'd,
The Dreamer's quaint dreams.

Mingles morals idyllic
With Samian fable,
Sage seasoned from cruets,
Of Plutarch's chaste table.

Pledges Zeus, Zoroaster,
Tastes Cana's glad cheer,
Sun's, globes, on his trencher,
The elements there.

Bowls of sunrise for breakfast
Brimful of the East,
Foaming flagons of frolic
His evening's gay feast.

Sov'reign solids of nature,
Solar seeds of the sphere,
Olympian viand
Surprising as rare.

Thus baiting his genius,
His wonderful word
Brings poets and sibyls
To sup at his board.

Feeds thus and thus fares he,
Speeds thus and thus cares he,
Thus faces and graces
Life's long euthanasies,

His gifts unabated,
Transfigured, translated —
The idealist prudent,
Saint, poet, priest, student,
Philosopher, he.

DR. CHANNING

Channing! my Mentor whilst my thought was
        young,
And I the votary of fair liberty, —
How hung I then upon thy glowing tongue,
And thought of love and truth as one with thee!
Thou wast the inspirer of a nobler life,
When I with error waged unequal strife,
And from its coils thy teaching set me free.
Be ye, his followers, to his leading true,
Nor privilege covet, nor the wider sway;
But hold right onward in his loftier way,
As best becomes, and is his rightful due.
If learning's yours, — gifts God doth least es-
        teem, —
Beyond all gifts was his transcendent view;
O realize his Pentecostal dream!

EMERSON

I

Misfortune to have lived not knowing thee!
'T were not high living, nor to noblest end,

Who, dwelling near, learned not sincerity,
Rich friendship's ornament that still doth lend
To life its consequence and propriety.
Thy fellowship was my culture, noble friend:
By the hand thou took'st me, and didst condescend
To bring me straightway into thy fair guild;
And life-long hath it been high compliment
By that to have been known, and thy friend styled,
Given to rare thought and to learning bent;
Whilst in my straits an angel on me smiled.
Permit me, then, thus honored, still to be
A scholar in thy university.

II

Hierophant, and lyrist of the soul!
Clear insight thine of universal mind;
While from its crypts the nascent Powers unroll,
And represent to consciousness the Whole.
Each in its order seeks its natural kind,
These latent or apparent, stir or sleep,
Watchful o'er widening fields of airy space,
Or slumbering sightless in the briny deep; —
Thou, far above their shows, servant of Grace,
Tread'st the bright way from Spirit down to
        Sense,
Interpreting all symbols to thy race, —

Commanding vistas of the fair Immense,
And glimpses upward far, where, sons of Heaven,
Sit in Pantheon throned the Sacred Seven.

III

Pleased, I recall those hours, so fair and free,
When all the long forenoons we two did toss
From lip to lip, in lively colloquy,
Plato, Plotinus, or famed schoolman's gloss,
Disporting in rapt thought and ecstasy.
Then by the tilting rail Millbrook we cross,
And sally through the fields to Walden wave,
Plunging within the cove, or swimming o'er;
Through woodpaths wending, he with gesture quick
Rhymes deftly in mid-air with circling stick,
Skims the smooth pebbles from the leafy shore,
Or deeper ripples raises as we lave;
Nor slumb'rous pillow touches at late night,
Till converse with the stars his eyes invite.

Henry David Thoreau

STANZAS

NATURE doth have her dawn each day,
  But mine are far between ;
Content, I cry, for, sooth to say,
  Mine brightest are, I ween.

For when my sun doth deign to rise,
  Though it be her noontide,
Her fairest field in shadow lies,
  Nor can my light abide.

Sometimes I bask me in her day,
  Conversing with my mate,
But if we interchange one ray,
  Forthwith her heats abate.

Through his discourse I climb and see
  As from some eastern hill,
A brighter morrow rise to me
  Than lieth in her skill.

As 't were two summer days in one,
  Two Sundays come together,

Our rays united make one sun,
    With fairest summer weather.

INSPIRATION

Whate'er we leave to God, God does,
    And blesses us ;
The work we choose should be our own,
    God leaves alone.

———

If with light head erect I sing,
    Though all the Muses lend their force,
From my poor love of anything,
    The verse is weak and shallow as its source.

But if with bended neck I grope,
    Listening behind me for my wit,
With faith superior to hope,
    More anxious to keep back than forward it ;

Making my soul accomplice there
    Unto the flame my heart hath lit,
Then will the verse for ever wear —
    Time cannot bend the line which God hath
      writ.

Always the general show of things
　　Floats in review before my mind,
And such true love and reverence brings,
　　That sometimes I forget that I am blind.

But now there comes unsought, unseen,
　　Some clear divine electuary,
And I, who had but sensual been,
　　Grow sensible, and as God is, am wary.

I hearing get, who had but ears,
　　And sight, who had but eyes before,
I moments live, who lived but years,
　　And truth discern, who knew but learning's
　　　　lore.

I hear beyond the range of sound,
　　I see beyond the range of sight,
New earths and skies and seas around,
　　And in my day the sun doth pale his light.

A clear and ancient harmony
　　Pierces my soul through all its din,
As through its utmost melody, —
　　Farther behind than they, farther within.

INSPIRATION

More swift its bolt than lightning is,
   Its voice than thunder is more loud,
It doth expand my privacies
   To all, and leave me single in the crowd.

It speaks with such authority,
   With so serene and lofty tone,
That idle Time runs gadding by,
   And leaves me with Eternity alone.

Now chiefly is my natal hour,
   And only now my prime of life,
Of manhood's strength it is the flower,
   'T is peace's end and war's beginning strife.

It comes in summer's broadest noon,
   By a grey wall or some chance place,
Unseasoning Time, insulting June,
   And vexing day with its presuming face.

Such fragrance round my couch it makes,
   More rich than are Arabian drugs,
That my soul scents its life and wakes
   The body up beneath its perfumed rugs.

Such is the Muse, the heavenly maid,
   The star that guides our mortal course,

Which shows where life's true kernel's laid,
 Its wheat's fine flower, and its undying force.

She with one breath attunes the spheres,
 And also my poor human heart,
With one impulse propels the years
 Around, and gives my throbbing pulse its start.

I will not doubt for evermore,
 Nor falter from a steadfast faith,
For though the system be turned o'er,
 God takes not back the word which once he
  saith.

I will not doubt the love untold
 Which not my worth nor want has bought,
Which wooed me young, and wooes me old,
 And to this evening hath me brought.

My memory I'll educate
 To know the one historic truth,
Remembering to the latest date
 The only true and sole immortal youth.

Be but thy inspiration given,
 No matter through what danger sought,

I 'll fathom hell or climb to heaven,
  And yet esteem that cheap which love has
    brought.

—————

    Fame cannot tempt the bard
      Who 's famous with his God,
    Nor laurel him reward
      Who has his Maker's nod.

MY PRAYER

GREAT God, I ask thee for no meaner pelf
Than that I may not disappoint myself;
That in my action I may soar as high
As I can now discern with this clear eye.

And next in value, which thy kindness lends,
That I may greatly disappoint my friends,
Howe'er they think or hope that it may be,
They may not dream how thou 'st distinguished me.

That my weak hand may equal my firm faith,
And my life practise more than my tongue saith;
    That my low conduct may not show,
      Nor my relenting lines,

That I thy purpose did not know,
Or overrated thy designs.

RUMORS FROM AN ÆOLIAN HARP

THERE is a vale which none hath seen,
Where foot of man has never been,
Such as here lives with toil and strife,
An anxious and a sinful life.

There every virtue has its birth,
Ere it descends upon the earth,
And thither every deed returns,
Which in the generous bosom burns.

There love is warm, and youth is young,
And poetry is yet unsung,
For Virtue still adventures there,
And freely breathes her native air.

And ever, if you hearken well,
You still may hear its vesper bell,
And tread of high-souled men go by,
Their thoughts conversing with the sky.

CONSCIENCE

CONSCIENCE is instinct bred in the house,
Feeling and Thinking propagate the sin
By an unnatural breeding in and in.
I say, Turn it out doors,
Into the moors.
I love a life whose plot is simple,
And does not thicken with every pimple,
A soul so sound no sickly conscience binds it,
That makes the universe no worse than 't
    finds it.
I love an earnest soul,
Whose mighty joy and sorrow
Are not drowned in a bowl,
And brought to life to-morrow;
That lives one tragedy,
And not seventy;
A conscience worth keeping,
Laughing not weeping;
A conscience wise and steady,
And for ever ready;
Not changing with events,
Dealing in compliments;

A conscience exercised about
Large things, where one *may* doubt.
I love a soul not all of wood,
Predestinated to be good,
But true to the backbone
Unto itself alone,
And false to none ;
Born to its own affairs,
Its own joys and own cares ;
By whom the work which God begun
Is finished, and not undone ;
Taken up where he left off,
Whether to worship or to scoff ;
If not good, why then evil,
If not good god, good devil.
Goodness ! — you hypocrite, come out of that,
Live your life, do your work, then take your
    hat.
I have no patience towards
Such conscientious cowards.
Give me simple laboring folk,
Who love their work,
Whose virtue is a song
To cheer God along.

THE INWARD MORNING

PACKED in my mind lie all the clothes
    Which outward nature wears,
And in its fashion's hourly change
    It all things else repairs.

In vain I look for change abroad,
    And can no difference find,
Till some new ray of peace uncalled
    Illumes my inmost mind.

What is it gilds the trees and clouds,
    And paints the heavens so gay,
But yonder fast-abiding light
    With its unchanging ray?

Lo, when the sun streams through the wood,
    Upon a winter's morn,
Where'er his silent beams intrude
    The murky night is gone.

How could the patient pine have known
    The morning breeze would come,

71

Or humble flowers anticipate
　　The insect's noonday hum, —

Till the new light with morning cheer
　　From far streamed through the aisles,
And nimbly told the forest trees
　　For many stretching miles?

I 've heard, within my inmost soul,
　　Such cheerful morning news,
In the horizon of my mind
　　Have seen such orient hues,

As in the twilight of the dawn,
　　When the first birds awake,
Are heard within some silent wood,
　　Where they the small twigs break,

Or in the eastern skies are seen,
　　Before the sun appears,
The harbinger of summer heats,
　　Which from afar he bears.

LINES

ALL things are current found
On earthly ground,
Spirits and elements
Have their descents.

Night and day, year on year,
High and low, far and near,
These are our own aspects,
These are our own regrets.

Ye gods of the shore,
Who abide evermore,
I see your far headland,
Stretching on either hand ;

I hear the sweet evening sounds
From your undecaying grounds ;
Cheat me no more with time,
Take me to your clime.

MY LIFE

My life is like a stroll upon the beach,
   As near the ocean's edge as I can go ;
My tardy steps its waves sometimes o'erreach,
   Sometimes I stay to let them overflow.

My sole employment is, and scrupulous care,
   To place my gains beyond the reach of tides,
Each smoother pebble, and each shell more rare,
   Which Ocean kindly to my hand confides.

I have but few companions on the shore :
   They scorn the strand who sail upon the
      sea ;
Yet oft I think the ocean they 've sailed o'er
   Is deeper known upon the strand to me.

The middle sea contains no crimson dulse,
   Its deeper waves cast up no pearls to view ;
Along the shore my hand is on its pulse,
   And I converse with many a shipwrecked
      crew.

74

Margaret Fuller

LIFE A TEMPLE

The temple round
Spread green the pleasant ground;
    The fair colonnade
Be of pure marble pillars made;
Strong to sustain the roof,
    Time and tempest proof;
Yet, amidst which, the lightest breeze
    Can play as it please;
    The audience hall
    Be free to all
    Who revere
The power worshipped here,
    Sole guide of youth,
    Unswerving Truth.
    In the inmost shrine
    Stands the image divine,
      Only seen
By those whose deeds have worthy been —
    Priestlike clean.
Those, who initiated are,

Declare,
As the hours
Usher in varying hopes and powers ;
It changes its face,
It changes its age,
Now a young, beaming Grace,
Now a Nestorian Sage :
But, to the pure in heart,
This shape of primal art
In age is fair,
In youth seems wise,
Beyond compare,
Above surprise ;
What it teaches native seems,
Its new lore our ancient dreams ;
Incense rises from the ground ;
Music flows around ;
Firm rest the feet below, clear gaze the eyes
above,
When Truth, to point the way through Life,
assumes the wand of Love ;
But, if she cast aside the robe of green,
Winter's silver sheen,
White, pure as light,
Makes gentle shroud as worthy weed as bridal
robe has been.

ENCOURAGEMENT

" I will not leave you comfortless "

O FRIEND divine, this promise dear
Falls sweetly on the weary ear!
Often, in hours of sickening pain,
It soothes me to thy rest again.

Might I a true disciple be,
Following thy footsteps faithfully,
Then should I still the succor prove
Of him who gave his life for love.

When this fond heart would vainly beat
For bliss that ne'er on earth we meet,
For perfect sympathy of soul,
For those such heavy laws control;

When, roused from passion's ecstasy,
I see the dreams that filled it fly,
Amid my bitter tears and sighs
Those gentle words before me rise.

With aching brows and feverish brain
The founts of intellect I drain,

77

And con with over-anxious thought
What poets sung and heroes wrought.

Enchanted with their deeds and lays,
I with like gems would deck my days;
No fires creative in me burn,
And, humbled, I to Thee return;

When blackest clouds around me rolled
Of skepticism drear and cold,
When love, and hope, and joy, and pride,
Forsook a spirit deeply tried;

My reason wavered in that hour,
Prayer, too impatient, lost its power;
From thy benignity a ray
I caught, and found the perfect day.

A head revered in dust was laid;
For the first time I watched my dead;
The widow's sobs were checked in vain,
And childhood's tears poured down like rain.

In awe I gazed on that dear face,
In sorrow, years gone by retrace,
When, nearest duties most forgot,
I might have blessed, and did it not!

Ignorant, his wisdom I reproved,
Heedless, passed by what most he loved,
Knew not a life like his to prize,
Of ceaseless toil and sacrifice.

No tears can now that hushed heart move,
No cares display a daughter's love,
The fair occasion lost, no more
Can thoughts more just to thee restore.

What can I do? And how atone
For all I 've done, and left undone?
Tearful I search the parting words
Which the belovèd John records.

" Not comfortless! "   I dry my eyes,
My duties clear before me rise, —
Before thou think'st of taste or pride,
See home affections satisfied!

Be not with generous thoughts content,
But on well-doing constant bent:
When self seems dear, self-seeking fair,
Remember this sad hour in prayer!

Though all thou wishest fly thy touch,
Much can one do who loveth much.

More of thy spirit, Jesus, give,
Not comfortless, though sad, to live.

And yet not sad, if I can know
To copy him who here below
Sought but to do his Father's will,
Though from such sweet composure still

My heart be far. Wilt thou not aid
One whose best hopes on thee are stayed?
Breathe into me thy perfect love,
And guide me to thy rest above!

SUB ROSA, CRUX

In times of old, as we are told,
When men more child-like at the feet
    Of Jesus sat, than now,
A chivalry was known more bold
    Than ours, and yet of stricter vow,
Of worship more complete.

Knights of the Rosy Cross, they bore
Its weight within the heart, but wore
Without, devotion's sign in glistening ruby bright;

The gall and vinegar they drank alone,
  But to the world at large would only own
The wine of faith, sparkling with rosy light.

They knew the secret of the sacred oil
  Which, poured upon the prophet's head,
Could keep him wise and pure for aye.
  Apart from all that might distract or soil,
  With this their lamps they fed,
Which burn in their sepulchral shrines unfading
      night and day.

  The pass-word now is lost
  To that initiation full and free;
    Daily we pay the cost
  Of our slow schooling for divine degree.
We know no means to feed an undying lamp;
Our lights go out in every wind or damp.

We wear the cross of ebony and gold,
  Upon a dark background a form of light,
A heavenly hope upon a bosom cold,
  A starry promise in a frequent night;
The dying lamp must often trim again,
For we are conscious, thoughtful, striving men.

Yet be we faithful to this present trust,
Clasp to a heart resigned the fatal must ;
Though deepest dark our efforts should enfold,
Unwearied mine to find the vein of gold;
Forget not oft to lift the hope on high ;
The rosy dawn again shall fill the sky.

And by that lovely light, all truth-revealed,
The cherished forms which sad distrust concealed,
Transfigured, yet the same, will round us stand,
The kindred angels of a faithful band ;
Ruby and ebon cross both cast aside,
No lamp is needed, for the night has died.

Happy be those who seek that distant day,
With feet that from the appointed way
        Could never stray ;
Yet happy too be those who more and more,
As gleams the beacon of that only shore,
        Strive at the laboring oar.

Be to the best thou knowest ever true,
    Is all the creed ;
Then, be thy talisman of rosy hue,
    Or fenced with thorns that wearing thou must
        bleed,

82

Or gentle pledge of Love's prophetic view,
    The faithful steps it will securely lead.

Happy are all who reach that shore,
    And bathe in heavenly day,
Happiest are those who high the banner bore,
    To marshal others on the way;
Or waited for them, fainting and way-worn,
    By burdens overborne.

DRYAD SONG

I AM immortal! I know it! I feel it!
    Hope floods my heart with delight!
Running on air, mad with life, dizzy, reeling,
Upward I mount, — faith is sight, life is feeling,
    Hope is the day-star of might!

It was thy kiss, Love, that made me immortal, —
    "'Kiss,' Love? Our lips have not met!"
Ah, but I felt thy soul through night's portal
Swoon on my lips at night's sweet, silent portal,
    Wild and as sweet as regret.

Come, let us mount on the wings of the morning,
    Flying for joy of the flight,

Wild with all longing, now soaring, now staying,
Mingling like day and dawn, swinging and sway-
     ing,
  Hung like a cloud in the light:
I am immortal! I feel it! I feel it!
  Love bears me up, love is might!

Chance cannot touch me! Time cannot hush me!
  Fear, Hope, and Longing, at strife,
Sink as I rise, on, on, upward forever,
Gathering strength, gaining breath, — naught can
     sever
  Me from the Spirit of Life!

Christopher Pearse Cranch

GNOSIS

THOUGHT is deeper than all speech,
　　Feeling deeper than all thought:
Souls to souls can never teach
　　What unto themselves was taught.

We are spirits clad in veils ;
　　Man by man was never seen ;
All our deep communing fails
　　To remove the shadowy screen.

Heart to heart was never known ;
　　Mind with mind did never meet ;
We are columns left alone
　　Of a temple once complete.

Like the stars that gem the sky,
　　Far apart though seeming near,
In our light we scattered lie ;
　　All is thus but starlight here.

What is social company
　　But a babbling summer stream?

What our wise philosophy
　　But the glancing of a dream?

Only when the Sun of Love
　　Melts the scattered stars of thought,
Only when we live above
　　What the dim-eyed world hath taught,

Only when our souls are fed
　　By the Fount which gave them birth,
And by inspiration led
　　Which they never drew from earth,

We, like parted drops of rain,
　　Swelling till they meet and run,
Shall be all absorbed again,
　　Melting, flowing into one.

CORRESPONDENCES

ALL things in Nature are beautiful types to the
　　soul that will read them;
　　Nothing exists upon earth, but for unspeakable
　　ends.

CORRESPONDENCES

Every object that speaks to the senses was meant
    for the spirit :
  Nature is but a scroll, — God's handwriting
    thereon.
Ages ago, when man was pure, ere the flood over-
    whelmed him,
  While in the image of God every soul yet lived,
Everything stood as a letter or word of a language
    familiar,
  Telling of truths which now only the angels can
    read.
Lost to man was the key of those sacred hiero-
    glyphics, —
  Stolen away by sin, — till with Jesus restored.
Now with infinite pains we here and there spell
    out a letter ;
  Now and then will the sense feebly shine
    through the dark.
When we perceive the light which breaks through
    the visible symbol,
  What exultation is ours ! we the discovery have
    made !
Yet is the meaning the same as when Adam lived
    sinless in Eden,
  Only long-hidden it slept and now again is re-
    stored.

Man unconsciously uses figures of speech every
    moment,
    Little dreaming the cause why to such terms he
        is prone, —
Little dreaming that everything has its own corre-
    spondence
    Folded within it of old, as in the body the
        soul.
Gleams of the mystery fall on us still, though
    much is forgotten,
    And through our commonest speech illumines the
        path of our thoughts.
Thus does the lordly sun shine out a type of the
    Godhead ;
    Wisdom and Love the beams that stream on a
        darkened world.
Thus do the sparkling waters flow, giving joy to
    the desert,
    And the great Fountain of Life opens itself to
        the thirst.
Thus does the word of God distil like the rain
    and the dew-drops,
    Thus does the warm wind breathe like to the
        Spirit of God,
And the green grass and the flowers are signs of
    the regeneration.

O thou Spirit of Truth! visit our minds once
more!
Give us to read, in letters of light, the language
celestial,
Written all over the earth, — written all over
the sky:
Thus may we bring our hearts at length to know
our Creator,
Seeing in all things around types of the Infinite
Mind.

THE OCEAN

" In a season of calm weather
Though inland far we be,
Our souls have sight of that immortal sea
That brought us hither,
Can in a moment travel thither,
And see the children sport upon the shore,
And hear the mighty waters rolling evermore."
WORDSWORTH.

TELL me, brother, what are we?
Spirits bathing in the sea
Of Deity!
Half afloat, and half on land,
Wishing much to leave the strand,
Standing, gazing with devotion,

Yet afraid to trust the ocean, —
Such are we.

Wanting love and holiness,
To enjoy the wave's caress ;
Wanting faith and heavenly hope,
Buoyantly to bear us up ;
Yet impatient in our dwelling,
When we hear the ocean swelling,
And in every wave that rolls
We behold the happy souls
Peacefully, triumphantly
Swimming on the smiling sea,
Then we linger round the shore,
Lovers of the earth no more.

Once, — 't was in our infancy, —
We were drifted by this sea
To the coast of human birth,
To this body and this earth ;
Gentle were the hands that bore
Our young spirits to the shore ;
Gentle lips that bade us look
Outward from our cradle-nook
To the spirit-bearing ocean
With such wonder and devotion,

As, each stilly Sabbath day
We were led a little way,
Where we saw the waters swell
Far away from inland dell,
And received with grave delight
Symbols of the Infinite : —
Then our home was near the sea ;
" Heaven was round our infancy ; " —
Night and day we heard the waves
Murmuring by us to their caves ; —
Floated in unconscious life
With no later doubts at strife,
Trustful of th' Upholding Power,
Who sustained us hour by hour.

Now we 've wandered from the shore,
Dwellers by the sea no more ;
Yet at times there comes a tone
Telling of the visions flown,
Soundings from the distant sea
Where we left our purity :
Distant glimpses of the surge
Lure us down to ocean's verge ;
There we stand with vague distress
Yearning for the measureless,
By half-wakened instincts driven,

Half loving earth, half loving heaven,
Fearing to put off and swim,
Yet impelled to turn to Him,
In whose life we live and move,
And whose very name is Love.

Grant me courage, Holy One,
To become indeed thy son,
And in thee, thou Parent-Sea,
Live and love eternally.

I IN THEE, AND THOU IN ME

I AM but clay in thy hands, but thou art the all-
loving artist;
Passive I lie in thy sight, yet in my selfhood I
strive
So to embody the life and love thou ever impartest
That in my sphere of the finite I may be truly
alive.

Knowing thou needest this form, as I thy divine
inspiration,
Knowing thou shapest the clay with a vision and
purpose divine,

So would I answer each touch of thy hand in its
    loving creation,
  That in my conscious life thy power and beauty
    may shine.

Reflecting the noble intent thou hast in forming
    thy creatures ;
  Waking from sense into life of the soul, and the
    image of thee ;
Working with thee in thy work to model human-
    ity's features
  Into the likeness of God, myself from myself I
    would free.

One with all human existence, no one above or
    below me ;
  Lit by thy wisdom and love, as roses are steeped
    in the morn ;
Growing from clay to statue, from statue to flesh,
    till thou know me
  Wrought into manhood celestial, and in thine
    image reborn.

So in thy love will I trust, bringing me sooner or later
  Past the dark screen that divides these shows of
    the finite from thee.

Thine, thine only, this warm dear life, O loving
    Creator!
  Thine the invisible future, born of the present,
    must be.

HUMAN HELPERS

PRAISE, praise ye the prophets, the sages
Who lived and who died for the ages;
The grand and magnificent dreamers;
The heroes, and mighty redeemers;
The martyrs, reformers, and leaders;
The voices of mystical Vedas;
The bibles of races long shrouded
Who left us their wisdom unclouded;
The truth that is old as their mountains,
But fresh as the rills from their fountains.

And praise ye the poets whose pages
Give solace and joy to the ages;
Who have seen in their marvellous trances
Of thought and of rhythmical fancies,
The manhood of Man in all errors;
The triumph of hope over terrors;
The great human heart ever pleading

SO FAR, SO NEAR

Its kindred divine, though misleading,
Fate held it aloof from the heaven
That to spirits untempted was given.

The creeds of the past that have bound us,
With visions of terror around us
Like dungeons of stone that have crumbled,
Beneath us lie shattered and humbled.
The tyranny mitred and crested,
Flattered and crowned and detested;
The blindness that trod upon Science;
   The bigotry Ignorance cherished;
The armed and the sainted alliance
   Of conscience and hate — they have perished,
Have melted like mists in the splendor
   Of life and of beauty supernal —
Of love ever watchful and tender,
   Of law ever one and eternal.

SO FAR, SO NEAR

Thou, so far, we grope to grasp thee —
Thou, so near, we cannot clasp thee —
Thou, so wise, our prayers grow heedless —
Thou, so loving, they are needless!

In each human soul thou shinest;
Human-best is thy divinest.
In each deed of love thou warmest;
Evil into good transformest.
Soul of all, and moving centre
Of each moment's life we enter.
Breath of breathing — light of gladness —
Infinite antidote of sadness; —
All-preserving ether flowing
Through the worlds, yet past our knowing.
Never past our trust and loving,
Nor from thine our life removing.
Still creating, still inspiring,
Never of thy creatures tiring.
Artist of thy solar spaces,
And thy humble human faces;
Mighty glooms and splendors voicing;
In thy plastic work rejoicing;
Through benignant law connecting
Best with best — and all perfecting,
Though all human races claim thee,
Thought and language fail to name thee,
Mortal lips be dumb before thee,
Silence only can adore thee!

William Ellery Channing

THOUGHTS

I.

THE Bible is a book worthy to read ;
The life of those great Prophets is the life we need,
From all delusive seeming ever freed.

Be not afraid to utter what thou art ;
'T is no disgrace to keep an open heart ;
A soul free, frank, and loving friends to aid,
Not even does this harm a gentle maid.

Strive as thou canst, thou wilt not value o'er
Thy life.   Thou standest on a lighted shore,
And from the waves of an unfathomed sea
The noblest impulses flow tenderly to thee ;
Feel them as they arise, and take them free.

> Better live unknown,
> No heart but thy own
> Beating ever near,
> To no mortal dear
> In thy hemisphere,
> Poor and wanting bread,

Steeped in poverty,
Than to be a dread,
Than to be afraid,
From thyself to flee;
For it is not living
To a soul believing,
To change each noble joy
Which our strength employs,
For a state half rotten
And a life of toys.
Better be forgotten
Than lose equipoise.

How shall I live?   In earnestness.
What shall I do?   Work earnestly.
What shall I give?   A willingness.
What shall I gain?   Tranquillity.
But do you mean a quietness
In which I act and no man bless?
Flash out in action infinite and free,
Action conjoined with deep tranquillity,
Resting upon the soul's true utterance,
And life shall flow as merry as a dance.

II.

Life is too good to waste, enough to prize;
Keep looking round with clear unhooded eyes;

THOUGHTS

Love all thy brothers, and for them endure
Many privations ; the reward is sure.

A little thing!   There is no little thing ;
Through all a joyful song is murmuring ;
Each leaf, each stem, each sound in winter drear
Has deepest meanings for an anxious ear.

Thou seest life is sad; the father mourns his wife
  and child ;
Keep in the midst of heavy sorrows a fair aspect
  mild.

A howling fox, a shrieking owl,
A violent distracting ghoul,
Forms of the most infuriate madness, —
These may not move thy heart to gladness,
But look within the dark outside,
Nought shalt thou hate and nought deride.

Thou meet'st a common man
With a delusive show of *can*.
His acts are petty forgeries of natural greatness,
That show a dreadful lateness
Of this life's mighty impulses ; a want of truthful
  earnestness ;

He seems, not does, and in that shows
    No true nobility, —
    A poor ductility,
That no proper office knows,
Not even estimation small of human woes.

    Be not afraid,
    His understanding aid
    With thy own pure content,
    On highest purpose bent.

Leave him not lonely,
For that his admiration
Fastens on self and seeming only;
Make a right dedication
Of all thy strength to keep
From swelling that so ample heap
Of lives abused, of virtue given for nought,
And thus it shall appear for all in nature hast
    thou wrought.
If thou unconsciously perform what 's good,
Like nature's self thy proper mood.

A life well spent is like a flower,
That had bright sunshine its brief hour;
It flourished in pure willingness;

Discovered strongest earnestness ;
Was fragrant for each lightest wind ;
Was of its own particular kind ; —
Nor knew a tone of discord sharp ;
Breathed alway like a silver harp ;
And went to immortality
A very proper thing to die.

CONTENT

WITHIN the unpainted cottage dwell
   The spirits of serene content,
As clear as from its moss-grown well
   Rises the crystal element.

Above, the elm, whose trunk is scarred
   With many a dint of stormy weather,
Rises, a sumptuous screen, debarred
   Of nothing that links life together.

Our common life may gratify
   More feelings than the rarest art,
For nothing can aspire so high
   As beatings of the human heart.

O! value then thy daily cheer,
  Poor pensioner on nature's store,
And clasp the least, and hold most dear
  What seemeth small, and add the more.

A POET'S HOPE

LADY, there is a hope that all men have
Some mercy for their faults, a grassy place
To rest in, and a flower-strewn, gentle grave;
Another hope which purifies our race,
That when that fearful bourn forever past,
They may find rest, — and rest so long to last.

I seek it not, I ask no rest forever,
My path is onward to the farthest shores, —
Upbear me in your arms, unceasing river,
That from the soul's clear fountain swiftly pours,
Motionless not, until the end is won,
Which now I feel has scarcely felt the sun.

To feel, to know, to soar unlimited,
'Mid throngs of light-winged angels sweeping far,
And pore upon the realms unvisited,
That tesselate the unseen unthought star,

102

To be the thing that now I feebly dream
Flashing within my faintest, deepest gleam.

Ah, caverns of my soul! how thick your shade,
Where flows that life by which I faintly see, —
Wave your bright torches, for I need your aid,
Golden-eyed demons of my ancestry!
Your son though blinded hath a light within,
A heavenly fire which ye from suns did win.

O Time! O Death! I clasp you in my arms,
For I can soothe an infinite cold sorrow,
And gaze contented on your icy charms,
And that wild snow-pile which we call to-mor-
        row;
Sweep on, O soft, and azure-lidded sky,
Earth's waters to your gentle gaze reply.

I am not earth-born, though I here delay;
Hope's child, I summon infiniter powers;
And laugh to see the mild and sunny day
Smile on the shrunk and thin autumnal hours;
I laugh, for hope hath happy place with me,
If my bark sink, 't is to another sea.

UNA

WE are centred deeper far
Than the eye of any star,
Nor can rays of long sunlight
Thread a pace of our daylight.
In thy form I see the day
Burning, of a kingdom higher,
In thy silver net-work play
Thoughts that to the Gods aspire;
In thy cheek I see the flame
Of the studious taper burn,
And thy Grecian eye might tame
Natures ashed in antique urn;
Yet with this lofty element
Flows a pure stream of gentle kindness,
And thou to life thy strength hast lent,
And borne profoundest tenderness
In thy Promethean fearless arm,
With mercy's love that would all angels charm.

So trembling meek, so proudly strong,
Thou dost to higher worlds belong,
Than where I sing this empty song:

Yet I, a thing of mortal kind,
Can kneel before thy pathless mind,
And see in thee what my mates say
Sank o'er Judea's hills one crimson day.
Yet flames on high the keen Greek fire,
And later ages rarefies,
And even on my tuneless lyre
A faint, wan beam of radiance dies.
And might I say what I have thought
Of thee, and those I love to-day,
Then had the world an echo caught
Of that intense, impassioned lay,
Which sung in those thy being sings,
And from the deepest ages rings.

TO THE POETS

They who sing the deeds of men,
From the earth upraise their fame,
Monuments in marble pen,
Keeping ever sweet their name,
Tell me, Poets, do I hear,
What you sing, with pious ear?

They who sing the maiden's kiss,
And the silver sage's thought,

Loveliness of inward bliss,
Or the graver learning taught,
Tell me, are your skies and streams
Real, or the shape of dreams?

Many rainy days must go,
Many clouds the sun obscure,
But your verses clearly show,
And your lovely thoughts more pure,
Mortals are we, but you are
Burning keenly like a star.

HYMN OF THE EARTH

MY highway is unfeatured air,
My consorts are the sleepless stars,
And men my giant arms upbear,
My arms unstained and free from scars.

I rest forever on my way,
Rolling around the happy sun,
My children love the sunny day,
But noon and night to me are one.

My heart has pulses like their own,
I am their Mother, and my veins

Though built of the enduring stone,
Thrill as do theirs with godlike pains.

The forests and the mountains high,
The foaming ocean and the springs,
The plains, — O pleasant company,
My voice through all your anthems rings.

Ye are so cheerful in your minds,
Content to smile, content to share,
My being in your chorus finds
The echo of the spheral air.

No leaf may fall, no pebble roll,
No drop of water lose the road,
The issues of the general Soul
Are mirrored in its round abode.

NATURE

I LOVE the universe, — I love the joy
Of every living thing.   Be mine the sure
Felicity, which ever shall endure ;
While passion whirls the madmen, as they toy,
To hate, I would my simple being warm

In the calm pouring sun ; and in that pure
And motionless silence, ever would employ
My best true powers, without a thought's annoy.
See and be glad !   O high imperial race,
Dwarfing the common attitude of strength,
Learn that ye stand on an unshaken base ;
Your powers will carry you to any length.
Up ! earnestly feel the gentle sunset beams ;
Be glad in woods, o'er sands ; by marsh, or streams.

PRIMAVERA, THE BREATH OF SPRING

WITH the rush and whirl of the fleet wild brook,
And the leap of the deer thro' the deep wild wood,
And the eyes of the flowers with that gentle look
That shines in the hearts of the truly good,
　　Dost thou refresh my weary mood.

And chantest thy hymn in the forest old,
Where the buds of the trees and their hearts of fire
Start to the song of thy harps of gold
As the maiden with a timid desire
　　At the thrill of her love's soft lyre.

Thou passest thy hand o'er the yellow fields
With a light caress like a mother's smile,

108

And the bright, soft grass to thy impulse yields
The green of its life that has slept the while;
    Sweet Spring! Thou knowest many a wile.

And joyfully, Spring, I welcome thee down
To the heavy hearts of my fellow-men;
To the windows dark of the thick-built town,
And the scholar who sits with his tiresome pen,
    In the shadow of his den.

Frolic, sweet flowers, along the wall-side,
Along the roadway where the foot-path goes,
And, ferns, in the pines where the rivers glide,
Be as cheerful as where the musk-rose blows,
    And gay as a child each thing that grows.

CONFESSIO AMANTIS

I STILL can suffer pain;
I strive and hope in vain;
My wounds may not all heal,
Nor time their depth reveal.

So dreamed I, of a summer day,
As in the oak's cool shade I lay,

And thought that shining, lightsome river
Went rippling, rippling on forever : —

That I should bend with pain,
Should sing and love in vain ;
That I should fret and pine,
And hopeless thought define.

I want a true and simple heart,
That asks no pleasure in a part,
But seeks the whole ; and finds the soul,
A heart at rest, in sure control.

I shall accept all I may have,
Or fine or foul, or rich or brave ;
Accept that measure in life's cup,
And touch the rim and raise it up.

Some drop of Time's strange glass it holds,
So much endurance it enfolds ;
Or base and small, or broadly meant,
I cannot spill God's element.

Dion or Cæsar drained no more,
Not Solon, nor a Plato's lore ;
So much had they the power to do,
So much hadst thou, and equals too.

James Freeman Clarke

HYMN AND PRAYER

INFINITE Spirit! who art round us ever,
    In whom we float as motes in summer sky,
May neither life nor death the sweet bond sever,
    Which joins us to our unseen Friend on high.

Unseen, yet not unfelt, if any thought
    Has raised our mind from earth, or pure desire,
Or generous act, or noble purpose brought,
    It is thy breath, O Lord, which fans the fire.

To me, the meanest of thy creatures, kneeling,
    Conscious of weakness, ignorance, sin, and
        shame,
Give such a force of holy thought and feeling,
    That I may live to glorify thy name;

That I may conquer base desire and passion,
    That I may rise o'er selfish thought and will,
O'ercome the world's allurement, threat, and fash-
      ion,
    Walk humbly, softly, leaning on thee still.

I am unworthy.   Yet for their dear sake,
  I ask, whose roots planted in me are found,
For precious vines are propped by rudest stake,
  And heavenly roses fed in darkest ground.

Beneath my leaves, though early fallen and faded,
    Young plants are warmed, they drink my
        branches' dew,
Let them not, Lord, by me be Upas-shaded,
    Make me for their sake firm, and pure, and
        true.

For their sake too, the faithful, wise, and bold,
    Whose generous love has been my pride and
        stay,
Those, who have found in me some trace of gold,
    For their sake purify my lead and clay.

And let not all the pains and toil be wasted,
    Spent on my youth by saints now gone to
        rest,
Nor that deep sorrow my Redeemer tasted,
    When on his soul the guilt of man was prest.

Tender and sensitive he braved the storm,
    That we might fly a well deservèd fate,

Poured out his soul in supplication warm,
　　Looked with his eyes of love on eyes of hate.

Let all this goodness by my mind be seen,
　　Let all this mercy on my heart be sealed,
Lord, if thou wilt, thy power can make me clean,
　　O speak the word, thy servant shall be healed.

Frederic Henry Hedge

QUESTIONINGS

HATH this world, without me wrought,
Other substance than my thought?
Lives it by my sense alone,
Or by essence of its own?
Will its life, with mine begun,
Cease to be when that is done,
Or another consciousness
With the self-same forms impress?

Doth yon fireball, poised in air,
Hang by my permission there?
Are the clouds that wander by
But the offspring of mine eye,
Born with every glance I cast,
Perishing when that is past?
And those thousand, thousand eyes,
Scattered through the twinkling skies,
Do they draw their life from mine,
Or of their own beauty shine?

Now I close my eyes, my ears,
And creation disappears;

Yet if I but speak the word,
All creation is restored.
Or, more wonderful, within
New creations do begin ;
Hues more bright and forms more rare
Than reality doth wear
Flash across my inward sense,
Born of the mind's omnipotence.

Soul! that all informest, say!
Shall these glories pass away?
Will those planets cease to blaze
When these eyes no longer gaze
And the life of things be o'er
When these pulses beat no more?

Thought! that in me works and lives, —
Life to all things living gives, —
Art thou not thyself, perchance,
But the universe in trance?
A reflection inly flung
By that world thou fanciedst sprung
From thyself — thyself a dream —
Of the world's thinking thou the theme.

Be it thus, or be thy birth
From a source above the earth —

Be thou matter, be thou mind,
In thee alone myself I find,
And through thee alone, for me,
Hath this world reality.
Therefore, in thee will I live,
To thee all myself will give,
Losing still, that I may find
This bounded self in boundless Mind.

John Sullivan Dwight

REST

SWEET is the pleasure
   Itself cannot spoil!
Is not true leisure
   One with true toil?

Thou that wouldst taste it,
   Still do thy best;
Use it, not waste it,
   Else 't is no rest.

Wouldst behold beauty
   Near thee? all round?
Only hath duty
   Such a sight found.

Rest is not quitting
   The busy career;
Rest is the fitting
   Of self to its sphere.

'T is the brook's motion,
   Clear without strife,

Fleeing to ocean
After its life.

Deeper devotion
Nowhere hath knelt;
Fuller emotion
Heart never felt.

'T is loving and serving
The Highest and Best!
'T is onwards, unswerving,
And that is true rest.

WORK WHILE IT IS DAY

WORK, and thou wilt bless the day
Ere the toil be done;
They that work not cannot pray,
Cannot feel the sun.
God is living, working still;
All things work and move;
Work, or lose the power to will,
Lose the power to love.

All the rolling planets glow
Bright as burning gold;

118

Should they pause, how soon they 'd grow
  Colorless and cold!
Joy and beauty, where were they,
  If the world stood still?
Like the world, thy law obey,
  And thy calling fill.

Love to labor owes its health,
  Will its willing powers;
Industry alone is wealth,
  What we do is ours.
Load the day with deeds of thought,
  While it waits for thee;
Then despatch it, richly fraught,
  To eternity.

MUSIC

Music 's the measure of the planet's motion,
  Heart-beat and rhythm of the glorious whole;
Fugue-like the streams roll, and the choral ocean
  Heaves in obedience to its high control.
Thrills through all hearts the uniform vibration,
  Starting from God, and felt from sun to sun;
God gives the key-note, Love to all creation;
  Join, O my soul, and let all souls be one!

Eliza Thayer Clapp

"THE FUTURE IS BETTER THAN THE PAST"

NOT where long-passed ages sleep
  Seek we Eden's golden trees;
In the future, folded deep,
  Are its mystic harmonies.

All before us lies the way,
  Give the past unto the wind;
All before us is the day,
  Night and darkness are behind.

Eden with its angels bold,
  Love and flowers and coolest sea,
Is not ancient story told,
  But a glowing prophecy.

In the spirit's perfect air,
  In the passions tame and kind,
Innocence from selfish care,
  The real Eden we shall find.

It is coming, it shall come,
　To the patient and the striving,
To the quiet heart at home,
　Thinking wise and faithful living.

When all error is worked out
　From the heart and from the life ;
When the sensuous is laid low,
　Through the spirit's holy strife ;

When the soul to sin hath died,
　True and beautiful and sound ;
Then all earth is sanctified,
　Up springs Paradise around.

Then shall come the Eden days,
　Guardian watch from seraph-eyes ;
Angels on the slanting rays,
　Voices from the opening skies,

From this spirit-land afar
　All disturbing force shall flee ;
Stir nor toil nor hope shall mar
　Its immortal unity.

ELIZA THAYER CLAPP

HYMN TO THE GOD OF STARS

GOD of those splendid stars ! I need
   Thy presence, need to know
That thou art God, my God indeed.
    Cold and far off they shine, they glow,
In their strange brightness, like to spirit's eyes,
Awful, intensely on my naked soul ;
Beautiful are they, but so strange, so cold,
I know them not : I shrink, I cling
Like a scared insect to this whirling ball,
Upon whose swelling lines I woke one morn,
Unknowing who I was or whence I came ;
And still I know not : fastened to its verge
By a resistless power, with it I speed
On its eternal way, and those strange eyes,
Those starry eyes, look ever on me thus ;
I wake, I sleep, but still they look on me,
Mild yet reproachful, beautiful but strange.
Visions are round me, — many moving things,
In clothing beautiful, soft and colored forms
With drooping heads caressing ; eyes so meek
And loving and appealing, but they hold
A nature strange and different, each enwrapt
In its own mortal mystery : near they are,

122

And yet how distant, — familiar, fond,
Yet strangers all!   I know not what they are.

And higher forms, from out whose mystic eyes,
Gracefully curved and vestal-like, obscured
By shading lashes, looks a being out,
That seems myself and is not, — kindred linked,
Yet most communionless: I know them not,
Nor they know me; nearest, yet most apart,
Moving in saddest mystery each to each,
Like spellbound souls that coldly meet in dreams
Which in some waking hour had intertwined.

Yet some, too, woven with me in a veil,
Viewless, but all-enduring, — kindred love:
Their eyes are on me like awakening light;
They touch my forehead, press my given hand,
Smile rare or oft, or sit most silently;
Yet all is understood, — the watchful care,
The sympathetic joy, and the unutterable wealth
Of helping tears, — all, all is understood:
Sure these are me; sure my affections, theirs,
Awe-stricken thoughts and over-rushing sins,
My hopes, my loves, my struggles, and my straits
Are theirs to bear, to know, to carry out,
To sift, to learn, to war and wrestle through,

Ah, no! oh, no! for every spirit round
There is a circle where no other comes.
Even when we lay our head upon the breast,
And pour our thoughts as liquid jewels out,
And feel the strength that comes from soul be-
     loved
Steal through our own as steals the living heat,
Nurture and bloom into the opening leaves;
Yet is the spirit lone, — its problem deep
No other may work out; its mystic way
No other wing may try: passionate hopes,
Mighty yet powerless, and most awful fears,
Its strength ne'er equal to the burden laid,
Longings to stop, yet eagerness to go,
Is its alone; a wall unscalable
Circuits the soul, — its fellows cannot pass;
The mother may not spoil the child, to take
The youthful burden on her willing heart,
Nor friend enfranchise friend.   Alone, alone
The soul must do its own immortal work;
The best beloved most distant are; the near
Far severed wide.   Soul knows not soul,
Not more than these unanswering stars divine.

     God of these stars sublime! I need
       Thy presence, need to know

That thou art God, my God indeed.
Shield me, 'mid thine innumerable worlds;
Give me some point where I may rest,
   While thy unceasing ages flow;
Hide me from thine irradiated stars,
And the far sadder light, untraceable
Of human eyes; for strangers are they all,
A wandering thought on the resistless air;
A questioning wail o'er the unlistening sea.
Recall, Eternal Source! and reassume
In thine own essence peace unutterable!

Charles Timothy Brooks

THE GREAT VOICES

A VOICE from the sea to the mountains,
    From the mountains again to the sea;
A call from the deep to the fountains:
    O spirit! be glad and be free!

A cry from the floods to the fountains,
    And the torrents repeat the glad song
As they leap from the breast of the mountains:
    O spirit! be free and be strong!

The pine forests thrill with emotion
    Of praise as the spirit sweeps by;
With the voice like the murmur of ocean
    To the soul of the listener they cry.

Oh, sing, human heart, like the fountains,
    With joy reverential and free;
Contented and calm as the mountains,
    And deep as the woods and the sea.

THE VOICE OF THE PINE

O TALL old pine ! O gloomy pine !
Old grim, gigantic, gloomy pine !
What is there in that voice of thine
That thrills so deep this heart of mine ?

Is it that in thy mournful sigh
Old years and voices long gone by,
And feelings that can never die,
Come thronging back on memory ?

Is it that in thy solemn roar
My listening spirit hears once more
The trumpet-music of the host
Of billows round my native coast ?

Or is it that I catch a sound
Of that more vast and dread profound, —
The soul's unfathomable sea,
The ocean of eternity ?

127

Ellen Hooper

BEAUTY AND DUTY

I SLEPT, and dreamed that life was beauty;
I woke, and found that life was duty.
Was thy dream then a shadowy lie?
Toil on, sad heart, courageously,
And thou shalt find thy dream to be
A noonday light and truth to thee.

THE STRAIGHT ROAD

BEAUTY may be the path to highest good,
And some successfully have it pursued.
Thou, who wouldst follow, be well warned to see
That way prove not a curvèd road to thee.
The straightest path perhaps which may be sought,
Lies through the great highway men call " I ought."

THE HEART'S CURE

" HEART, heart, lie still!
Life is fleeting fast,

Strife will soon be past."
"I cannot lie still,
Beat strong I will."

"Heart, heart, lie still!
Joy's but joy, and pain's but pain,
Either, little loss or gain."
"I cannot lie still,
Beat strong I will."

"Heart, heart, lie still!
Heaven is over all,
Rules this earthly ball."
"I cannot lie still,
Beat strong I will."

"Heart, heart, lie still!
Heaven's sweet grace alone
Can keep in peace its own."
"Let that me fill,
And I am still."

THE POET

HE touched the earth, a soul of flame,
His bearing proud, his spirit high,

Filled with the heavens from whence he came,
He smiled upon man's destiny.

Yet smiled as one who knew no fear,
And felt a secret strength within,
Who wondered at the pitying tear
Shed over human loss and sin.

Lit by an inward brighter light,
Than aught that round about him shone,
He walked erect through shades of night,
Clear was his pathway, but how lone!

Men gaze in wonder and in awe
Upon a form so like to theirs,
Worship the presence, yet withdraw,
And carry elsewhere warmer prayers.

Yet when the glorious pilgrim guest,
Forgetting once his strange estate,
Unloosed the lyre from off his breast
And strung its chords to human fate;

And gaily snatching some rude air,
Carolled by idle passing tongue,
Gave back the notes that lingered there,
And in heaven's tones earth's low lay sung;

Then warmly grasped the hand that sought
To thank him with a brother's soul,
And when the generous wine was brought,
Shared in the feast and quaffed the bowl ; —

Men laid their hearts low at his feet,
And sunned their being in his light,
Pressed on his way his steps to greet,
And in his love forgot his might.

And when, a wanderer long on earth,
On him its shadow also fell,
And dimmed the lustre of a birth,
Whose day-spring was from heaven's own well,

They cherished even the tears he shed,
Their woes were hallowed by his woe,
Humanity, half cold and dead,
Had been revived in genius' glow.

THE NOBLY BORN

WHO counts himself as nobly born
Is noble in despite of place,
And honors are but brands to one
Who wears them not with nature's grace.

The prince may sit with clown or churl,
  Nor feel his state disgraced thereby;
But he who has but small esteem
  Husbands that little carefully.

Then, be thou peasant, be thou peer,
  Count it still more thou art thine own;
Stand on a larger heraldry
  Than that of nation or of zone.

What though not bid to knightly halls?
  Those halls have missed a courtly guest;
That mansion is not privileged,
  Which is not open to the best.

Give honor due when custom asks,
  Nor wrangle for this lesser claim;
It is not to be destitute,
  To have the thing without the name.

Then dost thou come of gentle blood,
  Disgrace not thy good company; —
If lowly born, so bear thyself
  That gentle blood may come of thee.

Strive not with pain to scale the height
  Of some fair garden's petty wall,

But scale the open mountain side,
Whose summit rises over all.

THE GOAL

I SPRANG on life's free course, I tasked myself,
    And questioned what and how I meant to be;
And leaving far behind me power and pelf,
    I fixed a goal, — nor farther could I see.

For this I toiled, for this I ran and bled,
    And proudly thought upon my laurels there.
Lo, here I stand! all childlike to be led.
    My goal, self-fixed, has vanished into air.
I run, I toil, but see not all my way;
Ever more pure it shines into a perfect day.

WAYFARERS

How they go by — those strange and dreamlike
        men!
    One glance on each, one gleam from out each
        eye,
And that I never looked upon till now,
    Has vanished out of sight as instantly.

133

Yet in it passed there a whole heart and life,
  The only key it gave that transient look ;
But for this key its great event in time
  Of peace or strife to me a sealèd book.

THE CHIMNEY–SWEEP

  SWEEP ho !   Sweep ho !
He trudges on through sleet and snow.
Tired and hungry both is he,
And he whistles vacantly.
Sooty black his rags and skin,
But the child is fair within.
Ice and cold are better far
Than his master's curses are.
Mother of this little one,
Couldst thou see thy little son !

  Sweep ho !   Sweep ho !
He trudges on through sleet and snow.
At the great man's door he knocks,
Which the servant maid unlocks.
Now let in with laugh and jeer,
In his eye there stands a tear.
He is young, but soon will know
How to bear both word and blow.

A SPIRIT SHROUDED

Sweep ho! Sweep ho!
In the chimney sleet and snow.
Gladly should his task be done,
Were 't the last beneath the sun.
Faithfully it now shall be,
But, soon spent, down droppeth he.
Gazes round as in a dream,
Very strange, but true, things seem.
Led by a fantastic power
Which sets by the present hour,
Creeps he to a little bed,
Pillows there his aching head,
Falls into a sudden sleep
Like his childhood's sweet and deep;
But, poor thing! he does not know
Here he lay long years ago!

HYMN OF A SPIRIT SHROUDED

O GOD, who, in thy dear still heaven,
    Dost sit, and wait to see
The errors, sufferings, and crimes
    Of our humanity,
How deep must be thy causal love!
    How whole thy final care!

Since Thou, who rulest over all,
    Canst see, and yet canst bear.

ONE ABOUT TO DIE

Oh, melancholy liberty
Of one about to die —
When friends, with a sad smile,
And aching heart the while,
Every caprice allow,
Nor deem it worth while now
To check the restless will
Which death so soon shall still.

TO R. W. E.

Dry lighted soul, the ray that shines in thee,
    Shot without reflex from primeval sun,
We twine the laurel for the victories
    Which thou on thought's broad, bloodless field
        hast won.

Thou art the mountain where we climb to see
    The land our feet have trod this many a year.

136

THE WOOD-FIRE

Thou art the deep and crystal winter sky,
    Where noiseless, one by one, bright stars appear.

It may be Bacchus, at thy birth, forgot
    That drop from out the purple grape to press
Which is his gift to man, and so thy blood
    Doth miss the heat which ofttimes breeds excess.

But, all more surely do we turn to thee
    When the day's heat and blinding dust are o'er,
And cool our souls in thy refreshing air,
    And find the peace which we had lost before.

THE WOOD-FIRE

    THIS bright wood-fire
    So like to that which warmed and lit
    My youthful days — how doth it flit
    Back on the periods nigher,
Relighting and rewarming with its glow
The bright scenes of my youth — all gone out now.
How eagerly its flickering blaze doth catch
On every point now wrapped in time's deep shade,
Into what wild grotesqueness by its flash
And fitful checquering is the picture made!
    When I am glad or gay,

137

Let me walk forth into the brilliant sun,
And with congenial rays be shone upon;
When I am sad, or thought-bewitched would be,
Let me glide forth in moonlight's mystery,
But never, while I live this changeful life,
This past and future with all wonders rife,
Never, bright flame, may be denied to me
Thy dear, life-imaging, close sympathy.
What but my hopes shot upward e'er so bright?
What but my fortunes sank so low in night?

Why art thou banished from our hearth and hall,
Thou who art welcomed and beloved by all?
Was thy existence then too fanciful
For our life's common light, who are so dull?
Did thy bright gleam mysterious converse hold
With our congenial souls? secrets too bold?
Well, we are safe and strong, for now we sit
Beside a hearth where no dim shadows flit,
Where nothing cheers nor saddens, but a fire
Warms feet and hands — nor does to more aspire;
By whose compact, utilitarian heap,
The present may sit down and go to sleep,
Nor fear the ghosts who from the dim past walked,
And with us by the unequal light of the old wood-
      fire talked.

TO THE IDEAL

Ah! what avails it thus to dream of thee,
Thou life above me, and aspire to be
A dweller in thy air serene and pure;
I wake, and must this lower life endure.

Look no more on me with sun-radiant eyes,
Mine droop so dimmed, in vain my weak sense tries
To find the color of this world of clay, —
Its hue has faded, its light died away.

In charity with life, how can I live?
What most I want, does it refuse to give.
Thou, who hast laid this spell upon my soul,
Must be to me henceforth a hope and goal.

Away, thou vision! Now must there be wrought
Armor from life in which may yet be fought
A way to thee, — thy memory shall inspire,
Although thy presence is consuming fire.

As one who may not linger in the halls,
And fair domains of this ancestral home,

Goes forth to labor, yet resolves those walls,
Redeemed, shall see his old age cease to roam, —

So exile I myself, thou dream of youth,
Thou castle where my wild thoughts wandered free,
Yet, bear a heart, which, through its love and
      truth,
Shall earn a right to throb its last with thee.

To work! with heart resigned, and spirit strong,
Subdued by patient toil Time's heavy wrong;
Through nature's dullest, as her brightest ways
We will march onward, singing to thy praise.

Yet when our souls are in new forms arrayed,
Like thine, immortal, by immortal aid,
And with forgiving blessing stand beside
The clay in which they toiled and long were tried.

When comes that solemn "undetermined" hour,
Light of the soul's light! present be thy power;
And welcome be thou, as a friend who waits
With joy, a soul unsphered at heaven's gates.

Caroline Tappan

ART AND ARTIST

WITH dauntless eye the lofty one
   Moves on through life ;
Majestic as the mighty sun
   He knows no strife.

He sees the thought flow to the form,
   And rise like bubble bright ;
A moment of beauty, — and it is gone,
   Dissolved in light.

AFTERNOON

I LIE upon the earth and feed upon the sky,
Drink in the soft, deep blue, falling from on high.
Walnut boughs, all steeped in gold, quiver to and
    fro ;
Winds like spirits murmur, as through the air they
    go,
My soul is filled with joy and holy faith and love,
For noble friends on earth and angels pure above.

CAROLINE TAPPAN

LINES

You go to the woods — what there have you seen?
Quivering leaves glossy and green;
Lights and shadows dance to and fro,
Beautiful flowers in the soft moss grow.
Is the secret of these things known to you?
Can you tell what gives the flower its hue?
Why the oak spreads out its limbs so wide?
And the graceful grape-vine grows by its side?
Why clouds full of sunshine are piled on high?
What sends the wind to sweep through the sky?
No! the secret of Nature I do not know —
A poor groping child, through her marvels I go!

THE BROOK

All the eyes I ever knew
　　In this my strange life-dream,
Hazel, gray, and deepest blue,
　　Are mingled in this stream.

It wins its way into my soul,
　　Awakes each hidden feeling,

Gives me a rapture beyond control,
　High love fills all my being.

In earnest eyes I chiefly live,
　All words to me are naught,
For me they neither take nor give,
　In the eye the soul is caught.

And now to see all that I love,
　And have gazed at many an hour,
Blended together, — has heaven above
　A greater joy in store?

THE HERO

THOU hast learned the woes of all the world!
　From thine own longings and lone tears,
And now thy broad sails are unfurled,
　And all men hail thee with loud cheers.

The flowing sunlight is thy home,
　The billows of the sea are thine,
To all the nations shalt thou roam,
　Through every heart thy love shall shine.

The subtlest thought that finds its goal
   Far, far beyond the horizon's verge,
Oh, shoot it forth on arrows bold,
   The thoughts of men, on, on, to urge.

Toil not to free the slave from chains,
   Think not to give the laborer rest;
Unless rich beauty fills the plains,
   The free man wanders still unblest.

All men can dig, and hew rude stone,
   But thou must carve the frieze above;
And columned high, through thee alone,
   Shall rise our frescoed homes of love.

Charles Anderson Dana

HERZLIEBSTE

My love for thee hath grown as grows the flowers,
Earthly at first, fast rooted in the earth,
Yet, with the promise of a better birth,
Putting forth shoots of newly wakened powers,
Tender green hopes, dreams which no God makes
  ours ;
And then the stalk, fitted life's frosts to bear,
To brave the wildest tempest's wildest art,
The immovable resolution of the heart
Ready and armed a world of ills to dare ;
And then the flower, fairest of things most fair,
The flower divine of love imperishable,
That seeth in thee the sum of things that are,
That hath no eye for aught mean or unstable,
But ever trustful, ever prayerful, feeleth
The mysteries the Holy Ghost revealeth.

VIA SACRA

Slowly along the crowded street I go,
Marking with reverent look each passer's face,

Seeking and not in vain, in each to trace
That primal soul whereof he is the show.
For here still move, by many eyes unseen,
The blessed gods that erst Olympus kept.
Through every guise these lofty forms serene
Declare the all-holding life hath never slept,
But known each thrill that in man's heart hath
        been,
And every tear that his sad eyes have wept.
Alas for us! the heavenly visitants, —
We greet them still as most unwelcome guests
Answering their smile with hateful looks askance,
Their sacred speech with foolish, bitter jests;
But oh! what is it to imperial Jove
That this poor world refuses all his love?

ETERNITY

UTTER no whisper of thy human speech,
But in celestial silence let us tell
Of the great waves of God that through us swell,
Revealing what no tongue could ever teach;
Break not the omnipotent calm, even by a prayer,
Filled with Infinite, seek no lesser boon:

But with these pines, and with the all-loving moon,
Asking naught, yield thee to the Only Fair;
So shall these moments so divine and rare,
These passing moments of the soul's high noon,
Be of thy day the first pale blush of morn;
Clad in white raiment of God's newly born,
Thyself shalt see when the great world is made
That flows forever from a Love unstayed.

AD ARMA!

Oh loiterer, that dalliest with thy dreams,
Content to watch thyself in graceful ease,
While clang of steel burdens each passing breeze,
And all the air is radiant with its gleams;
Where noble hearts, as noble heart beseems,
Answer the world's great cry with earnest deeds,
Fulfilling thus their own most inward needs;
Is there no Spartan nerve in all thy frame
That feels the summons to that solemn field!
And canst thou then its sacred honors yield,
And the high guerdon of eternal fame,
For purple skies and wreaths of fading flowers,
And the short lustre of these flitting hours?

THE BANKRUPT

WITH what a deep and ever deeper joy
Upon that hope my life I prided all,
Thoughtless if woe which might that life destroy,
Or Heaven's own blessedness should thence befall;
Like as a venturous mariner that sails,
To seek those unknown Islands of the Blest;
Heedless that he who on that voyage fails,
Desolate seas and tossing storms must breast,
Till in his agony he gladly hails
The yawning wave that gulfs him down to rest;
So have I ventured thy dear love to gain,
And failing that I fail of all beside.
To my wrecked heart all voices speak in vain,
Duty and Hope, Friendship, and even Pride,
As sad, alone, indifferent, I wait
Invoking the last gloomy stroke of Fate.

George William Curtis

SPRING SONG

A BIRD sang sweet and strong
　　In the top of the highest tree;
He said, "I pour out my heart in song
　　For the summer that soon shall be!"

But deep in the shady wood,
　　Another bird sang, "I pour
My heart on the solemn solitude,
　　For the springs that return no more."

EBB AND FLOW

I WALKED beside the evening sea,
And dreamed a dream that could not be;
The waves that plunged along the shore
Said only — "Dreamer, dream no more."

But still the legions charged the beach;
Loud rang their battle-cry, like speech;

149

But changed was the imperial strain:
It murmured — " Dreamer, dream again ! "

I homeward turned from out the gloom, —
That sound I heard not in my room ;
But suddenly a sound, that stirred
Within my very breast, I heard.

It was my heart, that like a sea
Within my breast beat ceaselessly ;
But like the waves along the shore,
It said — " Dream on ! " and " Dream no more ! '

Jones Very

THE BARBERRY-BUSH

THE bush that has most berries and bitter fruit
Waits till the frost has turned its green leaves red,
Its sweetened berries will thy palate suit,
And thou mayst find e'en there a homely bread;
Upon the hills of Salem scattered wide,
Their yellow blossoms gain the eye in Spring;
And straggling e'en upon the turnpike's side,
Their ripened branches to your hand they bring;
I 've plucked them oft in boyhood's early hour,
That then I gave such name, and thought it true;
But now I know that other fruit as sour
Grows on what now thou callest *Me* and *You*;
Yet wilt thou wait the autumn that I see,
Will sweeter taste than these red berries be.

THE PRAYER

WILT Thou not visit me?
The plant beside me feels Thy gentle dew;

And every blade of grass I see,
From Thy deep earth its quickening moisture
    drew.

Wilt Thou not visit me?
Thy morning calls on me with cheering tone;
    And every hill and tree
Lends but one voice, the voice of Thee alone.

Come, for I need Thy love,
More than the flower the dew, or grass the rain;
    Come, gently as Thy holy dove;
And let me in Thy sight rejoice to live again.

I will not hide from them,
When Thy storms come, though fierce may be
    their wrath;
    But bow with leafy stem,
And strengthened follow on Thy chosen path.

Yes, Thou wilt visit me,
Nor plant nor tree Thine eye delights so well,
    As when from sin set free
My spirit loves with Thine in peace to dwell.

THE PRESENCE

I sit within my room, and joy to find
That Thou who always lov'st art with me here,
That I am never left by Thee behind,
But by thyself Thou keep'st me ever near ;
The fire burns brighter when with Thee I look,
And seems a kinder servant sent to me ;
With gladder heart I read Thy holy book,
Because Thou art the eyes by which I see ;
This aged chair, that table, watch and door
Around in ready service ever wait ;
Nor can I ask of Thee a menial more
To fill the measure of my large estate,
For Thou thyself, with all a father's care,
Where'er I turn, art ever with me there.

THE SON

Father, I wait thy word. The sun doth stand
Beneath the mingling line of night and day,
A listening servant, waiting thy command
To roll rejoicing on its silent way ;

The tongue of time abides the appointed hour,
Till on our ear its solemn warnings fall;
The heavy cloud withholds the pelting shower,
Then every drop speeds onward at thy call;
The bird reposes on the yielding bough,
With breast unswollen by the tide of song;
So does my spirit wait thy presence now
To pour thy praise in quickening life along,
Chiding with voice divine man's lengthened sleep,
While round the Unuttered Word and Love their
      vigils keep.

THE SPIRIT LAND

FATHER! Thy wonders do not singly stand,
Nor far removed where feet have seldom strayed;
Around us ever lies the enchanted land
In marvels rich to Thine own sons displayed;
In finding Thee are all things round us found;
In losing Thee are all things lost beside;
Ears have we, but in vain strange voices sound,
And to our eyes the vision is denied;
We wander in the country far remote,
'Mid tombs and ruined piles in death to dwell;
Or on the records of past greatness dote,

And for a buried soul the living sell ;
While on our path bewildered falls the night
That ne'er returns us to the fields of light.

THE VIOLET

THOU tellest truths unspoken yet by man,
By this thy lonely home and modest look ;
For he has not the eyes such truths to scan,
Nor learns to read from such a lowly book.
With him it is not life firm-fixed to grow
Beneath the outspreading oaks and rising pines,
Content this humble lot of thine to know,
The nearest neighbor of the creeping vines ;
Without fixed root he cannot trust like thee
The rain will know the appointed hour to fall,
But fears lest sun or shower may hurtful be,
And would delay, or speed them with his call ;
Nor trust like thee, when wintry winds blow cold,
Whose shrinking form the withered leaves en-
    fold.

THE IDLER

I IDLE stand, that I may find employ,
Such as my Master when He comes will give ;

I cannot find in mine own work my joy,
But wait, although in waiting I must live ;
My body shall not turn which way it will,
But stand till I the appointed road can find,
And journeying so His messages fulfil,
And do at every step the work designed.
Enough for me, still day by day to wait
Till Thou who form'st me find'st me too a
    task :
A cripple lying at the rich man's gate,
Content for the few crumbs I get to ask ;
A laborer but in heart, while bound my hands
Hang idly down still waiting Thy commands.

THE LIGHT FROM WITHIN

I saw on earth another light
    Than that which lit my eye
Come forth as from my soul within,
    And from a higher sky.

Its beams shone still unclouded on,
    When in the farthest west
The sun I once had known had sunk
    Forever to his rest.

And on I walked, though dark the night,
  Nor rose his orb by day;
As one who by a surer guide
  Was pointed out the way.

'T was brighter far than noonday's beam;
  It shone from God within,
And lit, as by a lamp from heaven,
  The world's dark track of sin.

HEALTH OF BODY DEPENDENT ON THE SOUL

NOT from the earth, or skies,
  Or seasons as they roll,
Come health and vigor to the frame,
  But from the living soul.

Is this alive to God,
  And not the slave to sin?
Then will the body, too, receive
  Health from the soul within.

But if disease has touched
  The spirit's inmost part,

157

In vain we seek from outward things
  To heal the deadly smart.

The mind, the heart unchanged,
  Which clouded e'en our home,
Will make the outward world the same
  Where'er our feet may roam.

The fairest scenes on earth,
  The mildest, purest sky,
Will bring no vigor to the step,
  No lustre to the eye.

For He who formed our frame
  Made man a perfect whole,
And made the body's health depend
  Upon the living soul.

THE SILENT

THERE is a sighing in the wood,
  A murmur in the beating wave,
The heart has never understood
  To tell in words the thoughts they gave.

Yet oft it feels an answering tone,
  When wandering on the lonely shore ;

And could the lips its voice make known,
  'T would sound as does the ocean's roar.

And oft beneath the windswept pine
  Some chord is struck the strain to swell;
Nor sounds nor language can define, —
  'T is not for words or sounds to tell.

'T is all unheard, that Silent Voice,
  Whose goings forth, unknown to all,
Bids bending reed and bird rejoice,
  And fills with music Nature's hall.

And in the speechless human heart
  It speaks, where'er man's feet have trod;
Beyond the lips' deceitful art,
  To tell of Him, the Unseen God.

NATURE

THE bubbling brook doth leap when I come by,
Because my feet find measure with its call;
The birds know when the friend they love is nigh,
For I am known to them, both great and small;
The flowers that on the lovely hillside grow

Expect me there when Spring their bloom has
 given;
And many a tree and bush my wanderings know,
And e'en the clouds and silent stars of heaven;
For he who with his Maker walks aright,
Shall be their lord, as Adam was before;
His ear shall catch each sound with new delight,
Each object wear the dress which then it wore;
And he, as when erect in soul he stood,
Hear from his Father's lips that all is good.

Theodore Parker

THE HIGHER GOOD

FATHER, I will not ask for wealth or fame,
Though once they would have joyed my carnal sense:
I shudder not to bear a hated name,
Wanting all wealth, myself my sole defence.
But give me, Lord, eyes to behold the truth;
A seeing sense that knows the eternal right;
A heart with pity filled, and gentlest ruth;
A manly faith that makes all darkness light:
Give me the power to labor for mankind;
Make me the mouth of such as cannot speak;
Eyes let me be to groping men and blind;
A conscience to the base; and to the weak
Let me be hands and feet; and to the foolish,
        mind;
And lead still further on such as thy kingdom seek.

THE WAY, THE TRUTH, THE LIFE

O THOU great Friend to all the sons of men,
Who once appear'dst in humblest guise below,

Sin to rebuke, to break the captive's chain,
To call thy brethren forth from want and woe! —
Thee would I sing.   Thy truth is still the light
Which guides the nations groping on their way,
Stumbling and falling in disastrous night,
Yet hoping ever for the perfect day.
Yes, thou art still the life ; thou art the way
The holiest know, — light, life, and way of heaven ;
And they who dearest hope and deepest pray
Toil by the truth, life, way that thou hast given ;
And in thy name aspiring mortals trust
To uplift their bleeding brothers rescued from the
        dust.

Samuel Gray Ward

THE CONSOLERS

CONSOLERS of the solitary hours
When I, a pilgrim, on a lonely shore
Sought help, and found none, save in those high
      powers
That then I prayed might never leave me more!
There was the blue, eternal sky above,
There was the ocean silent at my feet,
There was the universe — but nought to love ;
The universe did its old tale repeat.
Then came ye to me, with your healing wings,
And said, " Thus bare and branchless must thou be,
Ere thou couldst feel the wind from heaven that
      springs."
And now again fresh leaves do bud for me, —
Yet let me feel that still the spirit sings
In quiet song, coming from heaven free.

THE SHIELD

THE old man said, " Take thou this shield, my son,
Long tried in battle, and long tried by age,

Guarded by this thy fathers did engage,
Trusting to this the victory they have won."

Forth from the tower Hope and Desire had built,
In youth's bright morn I gazed upon the plain, —
There struggled countless hosts, while many a
    stain
Marked where the blood of brave men had been
    spilt.

With spirit strong I buckled to the fight,
What sudden chill rushes through every vein?
Those fatal arms oppress me — all in vain
My fainting limbs seek their accustomed might.

Forged were those arms for men of other mould;
Our hands they fetter, cramp our spirits free:
I throw them on the ground, and suddenly
Comes back my strength — returns my spirit
    bold.

I stand alone, unarmed, yet not alone;
Who heeds no law but that within he finds,
Trusts his own vision, not to other minds,
He fights with thee — Father, aid thou thy
    son.

David Atwood Wasson

IDEALS

ANGELS of growth, of old in that surprise
Of your first vision, wild and sweet,
   I poured in passionate sighs
   My wish unwise
That ye descend my heart to meet, —
   My heart so slow to rise !

Now thus I pray : Angelic be to hold
In heaven your shining poise afar,
   And to my wishes bold
   Reply with cold
Sweet invitation, like a star
   Fixed in the heavens old.

Did ye descend, what were ye more than I ?
Is 't not by this ye are divine, —
   That, native to the sky,
   Ye cannot hie
Downward, and give low hearts the wine
   That should reward the high ?

Weak, yet in weakness I no more complain
Of your abiding in your places;
   Oh, still, howe'er my pain
    Wild prayers may rain,
   Keep pure on high the perfect graces,
    That, stooping, could but stain!

Not to content our lowness, but to lure
And lift us to your angelhood,
   Do your surprises pure
    Dawn far and sure
   Above the tumult of young blood,
    And starlike there endure.

Wait there, — wait, and invite me while I climb;
For see, I come! — but slow, but slow!
   Yet ever as your chime,
    Soft and sublime,
Lifts at my feet, they move, they go
    Up the great stair of time.

SEEN AND UNSEEN

THE wind ahead, the billows high,
A whited wave, but sable sky,

And many a league of tossing sea
Between the hearts I love and me.

The wind ahead! day after day
These weary words the sailors say;
To weeks the days are lengthening now, —
Still mounts the surge to meet our prow.

Through longing day and lingering night,
I still accuse Time's lagging flight,
Or gaze out o'er the envious sea,
That keeps the hearts I love from me.

Yet, ah! how shallow is my grief!
How instant is the deep relief!
And what a hypocrite am I,
To feign forlorn, to 'plain and sigh!

The wind ahead!   The wind is free!
For evermore it favoreth me, —
To shores of God still blowing fair,
O'er seas of God my bark doth bear.

This surging brine *I* do not sail;
This blast adverse is not my gale;
'T is here I only seem to be,
But really sail another sea, —

Another sea, pure sky its waves,
Whose beauty hides no heaving graves;
A sea all haven, whereupon
No helpless bark to wreck has gone.

The winds that o'er my ocean run
Reach through all worlds beyond the sun;
Through life and death, through fate, through time,
Grand breaths of God they sweep sublime.

Eternal trades, they cannot veer,
And, blowing, teach us how to steer;
And well for him whose joy, whose care,
Is but to keep before them fair.

O thou God's mariner, heart of mine!
Spread canvas to the airs divine!
Spread sail! and let thy Fortune be
Forgotten in thy Destiny.

For Destiny pursues us well,
By sea, by land, through heaven or hell;
It suffers Death alone to die,
Bids Life all change and chance defy.

Would earth's dark ocean suck thee down?
Earth's ocean thou, O Life! shalt drown;

Shalt flood it with thy finer wave,
And, sepulchred, entomb thy grave!

Life loveth life and good, then trust
What most the spirit would, it must ;
Deep wishes in the heart that be,
Are blossoms of Necessity.

A thread of Law runs through thy prayer,
Stronger than iron cables are ;
And Love and Longing toward their goal
Are pilots sweet to guide the soul.

So Life must live, and Soul must sail,
And Unseen over Seen prevail ;
And all God's argosies come to shore,
Let ocean smile, or rage or roar.

And so, 'mid storm or calm, my bark
With snowy wake still nears her mark ;
Cheerly the trades of being blow,
And sweeping down the wind I go.

ALL 'S WELL

SWEET-VOICÈD Hope, thy fine discourse
    Foretold not half life's good to me ;

Thy painter, Fancy, hath not force
    To show how sweet it is to be!
        Thy witching dream
        And pictured scheme
To match the fact still want the power;
        Thy promise brave
        From birth to grave
Life's bloom may beggar in an hour.

Ask and receive, — 't is sweetly said;
    Yet what to plead for know I not;
For Wish is worsted, Hope o'ersped,
    And aye to thanks returns my thought.
        If I would pray,
        I 've naught to say
But this, that God may be God still,
        For Him to live
        Is still to give,
And sweeter than my wish His will.

O wealth of life beyond all bound!
    Eternity each moment given!
What plummet may the Present sound?
    Who promises a future heaven?
        Or glad, or grieved,
        Oppressed, relieved,

In blackest night, or brightest day,
    Still pours the flood
    Of golden good,
And more than heart-full fills me aye.

My wealth is common ; I possess
   No petty province, but the whole;
What 's mine alone is mine far less
   Than treasure shared by every soul.
    Talk not of store
    Millions or more, —
Of values which the purse may hold, —
    But this divine !
    I own the mine
Whose grains outweigh a planet's gold.

I have a stake in every star,
   In every beam that fills the day;
All hearts of men my coffers are,
   My ores arterial tides convey;
    The fields, the skies,
    The sweet replies
Of thought to thought are my gold-dust, —
    The oaks, the brooks,
    And speaking looks
Of lovers' faith and friendship's trust.

Life's youngest tides joy-brimming flow
  For him who lives above all years,
Who all-immortal makes the Now,
    And is not ta'en in Time's arrears;
      His life 's a hymn
      The seraphim
Might hark to hear or help to sing,
    And to his soul
    The boundless whole
Its bounty all doth daily bring.

" All time is mine," the sky-soul saith;
  " The wealth I am, must thou become;
Richer and richer, breath by breath, —
    Immortal gain, immortal room ! "
      And since all his
      Mine also is,
Life's gift outruns my fancies far,
    And drowns the dream
    In larger stream,
As morning drinks the morning-star.

LOVE AGAINST LOVE

As unto blowing roses summer dews,
Or morning's amber to the tree-top choirs,

So to my bosom are the beams that use
To rain on me from eyes that love inspires.
Your love, — vouchsafe it, royal-hearted few,
And I will set no common price thereon,
O, I will keep, as heaven his holy blue,
Or night her diamonds, that dear treasure won.
But aught of inward faith must I forego,
Or miss one drop from truth's baptismal hand,
Think poorer thoughts, pray cheaper prayers, and
       grow
Less worthy trust, to meet your heart's demand, —
Farewell! Your wish I for your sake deny:
Rebel to love, in truth to love, am I.

ROYALTY

THAT regal soul I reverence, in whose eyes
Sufficeth not all worth the city knows
To pay that debt which his own heart he owes;
For less than level to his bosom rise
The low crowd's heaven and stars: above their
       skies
Runneth the road his daily feet have pressed;
A loftier heaven he beareth in his breast,
And o'er the summits of achieving hies

173

With ne'er a thought of merit or of meed;
Choosing divinest labors through a pride
Of soul, that holdeth appetite to feed
Ever on angel-herbage, nought beside;
Nor praises more himself for hero-deed
Than stones for weight, or open seas for tide.

Sydney Henry Morse

TWO MOODS

I.

" THE Truth shall bind," quoth he ;
" No fetter else.   Oh! free
My mind shall rove, and bring
Me home on buoyant wing
The boldest thought that flies :
Blest freedom else unknown.
All shorn the soul denies
All beauty thus to own."

II.

Then spoke a voice in gentler strain,
Yet chanting still the high refrain :
" Nor rove will I to clip the wing
Of thoughts that fly and gaily sing.
Home, home I hie, all free to list
The silent song I ne'er resist."

OPEN SECRET

NOT through Nature shineth
  Godhead fair and free ;
'T is the Heart divineth
  What the God must be.

Nature all concealing,
  Dim her outer light,
Finite forms revealing,
  Not the infinite.

All the Godhead's planning
  Not with striving learn —
Inner eye — Heart scanning —
  Sees the God-bush burn.

SUNDERED

I CHALLENGE not the oracle
  That drove you from my board :
I bow before the dark decree
  That scatters as I hoard.

SUNDERED

Ye vanished like the sailing ships
   That ride far out at sea:
I murmur, as your farewell dies,
   And your forms float from me.

Ah! ties are sundered in this hour,
   No tide of fortune rare
Shall bring me hearts I owned before,
   And my love's loss repair.

When voyagers make a foreign port,
   And leave their precious prize,
Returning home, they bear for freight
   A bartered merchandise.

Alas! when ye come back to me,
   And come not as of yore,
But with your alien wealth and peace,
   Can we be lovers more?

I gave you up to go your ways,
   O you whom I adored!
Love hath no ties but Destiny
   Shall cut them with a sword.

TILL LOVE BE WHOLE

THE soul I dwell within
Forgets my load of sin,
  And circles me
  With amorous glee,
To win my first faint smile
Of love that bodes no guile ; —
Unfolds my heart the while,
  And sets me free.

Delights she to surprise
Me with some thought that hies
  To heaven straightway :
  Then all the day
I wander o'er the earth,
And find not half its worth ;
Yet lose I not my mirth,
  And pray, and pray.

Oh ! I am precious seed
Thus planted for her meed :
  My offish ways
  And long delays

She takes no notice of,
But steadily doth move
Upon my heart with love,
    Nor doubt displays.

Now I shall make return,
And my love's taper burn
    For my good soul,
    As towards the goal
My steps I hourly bend;
And to the flame yet lend
Increase, far to the end,
    Till love be whole?

THE WAY

THEY find the way who linger where
The soul finds fullest life;
The battle brave is carried on
By all who wait, and waiting, dare
Deem each day's least that's fitly done
A victory worthy to be won,
Nor seek their gain with strife.

WAIFS

GIRD thee, gird thee, soldier strong!
Gird thee with the hate of wrong, —
Gird thee with a love that smites
Down the hate of him who fights!
Victory be his as thine,
Soldier strong, whose face doth shine!

Erring world, sweet Charity
Veileth all thy sins that be :
She forgives e'en darkest crime,
She, with vision reaching far,
Sees the land whose glories are
Fair fulfilments of all time.

God wists not to hear thee pray,
When thou 'st somewhat wise to say ;
Finite wisdom blocks the way.
Better far thou speak'st no word —
Only let thy heart be heard.

SERVICE

FRET not that the day is gone,
And thy task is still undone.

'T was not thine, it seems, at all :
Near to thee it chanced to fall,
Close enough to stir thy brain,
And to vex thy heart in vain.
Somewhere, in a nook forlorn,
Yesterday a babe was born :
He shall do thy waiting task ;
All thy questions he shall ask,
And the answers will be given,
Whispered clearly out of heaven.
His shall be no stumbling feet,
Failing where they should be fleet ;
He shall hold no broken clue ;
Friends shall unto him be true ;
Men shall love him ; falsehood's aim
Shall not shatter his good name.
Day shall nerve his arm with light,
Slumber soothe him all the night ;
Summer's peace and winter's storm
Help him all his will perform.
'T is enough of joy for thee
His high service to foresee.

THE VICTORY

To do the tasks of life, and be not lost;
  To mingle, yet dwell apart;
To be by roughest seas how rudely tossed,
  Yet bate no jot of heart;

To hold thy course among the heavenly stars,
  Yet dwell upon the earth;
To stand behind Fate's firm-laid prison bars,
  Yet win all Freedom's worth!

John Weiss

BLEST SPIRIT OF MY LIFE

Blest spirit of my life, oh, stay!
  Let not this rapture vanish soon;
For thus my earth is snatched away,
  And lifted into heaven's noon.

How clear the vision! how serene
  The air through which my words aspire!
My narrow clay they leave to glean
  In fields of infinite desire.

Oh, greatest grief of many days,
  It is that thou, my heaven, art
So far, so faintly come the rays
  That kindle heaven in my heart.

To-day a prisoner on leave
  Am I: must I to bounds return?
Then make me blest that I can grieve,
  And satisfied that I can yearn.

Thou Light, that makest lesser lights
   To shine, burn up my cloudy sky!
To morning change my frequent nights;
   Drop planets to me from on high.

My hope is wide to take them in,
   Deeper than sight do I adore!
I am a little sail to win
   In thy great breath my native shore.

SAADI'S THINKING

SUCH a noon as Thought has made!
In my soul no spot of shade;
Least and greatest lying plain,
Hope of mystery was vain.

Like a savage creature's scent
To its game my daylight went;
Water hid beneath the sod
Sooner 'scapes divining rod.

All day staring like a noon
Sight must hie to shelter soon;
From the drooping lid must creep
Forth the outer edge of sleep.

As I lose my perfect gaze,
And the headlands gather haze,
Blushes through the clearness creep,
Showing it is also deep.

And my thought returns to me,
Like the diver from a sea,
Purpled with the shells he had, —
Tired and faint, but purple-clad.

Falls to dreaming all the sky,
Stirred by thoughts less palpably, —
Noontide broken into stars,
Vision checked by twilight bars.

Would you mystery receive,
And in miracle believe,
Wading out until some sea
Lifts the heart and sets it free, —

Then let Thought be shod with air,
Put on daylight for its wear —
Colorless and limpid laws:
In them stars and twilights pause.

MY TWO QUESTS

I.

Oh, many trees watch East,
And many trees ensnare the West, —
Those to drip with dawning golden,
These to keep the sunsets holden ;
Yet of all I love them least
That fail to nod above my quest.

Oh, many hills watch North,
And many in the South are faint, —
These to hold aloft the clearness,
These to bear away the nearness ;
Yet to all I wander loth,
To all save those my longings paint.

Oh, many flowers make sweet,
In many autumn fields, the grass.
Some to old resorts cajole me,
New surprises some would dole me ;
None of them can draw my feet,
Save those which smile to see her pass.

186

Oh, many paths invite
To beauties of the sky and land.
East and West the earth is tender,
North and South bend bows of splendor;
All the paths to me are trite,
Save one that leads me to her hand.

Oh, many days are born,
Both sweet and grave within them stir;
Perfect climes that have for ages
Been to kings and queens the pages;
But for all I have a scorn,
Save those which leap at sight of her.

Oh, many landscapes wait,
Tongue-tied, till thoughts release their word;
Thoughts like champions that travel,
Captives loose and charms unravel:
Best endowed of all but prate
Unless her mood has one preferred.

II.

Days I 've waited for my friend;
   Near yet absent waited He:
Time and chance did not attend,
   Nor a look to set me free.

Not a meeting of the eyes,
   Nor a touch of hands that groped
Through each hour's dull enterprise
   Toward the thrill for which we hoped.

Wainscoted with care the walls
   Are past which I feel my way.
Dark of absence deeper falls;
   Still I fumble, still I stay.

At a sudden turn, when least
   We surmised our hearts were near,
All the doubt, the strangeness, ceased;
   In a moment, dazzling clear.

Solid walls were built of mist,
   And our rapture burnt them down;
And the flash by which we kissed
   Seemed a sun for all the town,

Seemed to kindle every hearth,
   To consume each doubt and care,
Blaze along the common path,
   No reserve or dread to spare.

Thoughts that struggled from the slime,
   Nile-bred forms to gain their feet,

Suited with their perfect rhyme,
  Trooping came along the street ;

And I breathed them from the air ;
  Saw them, armored by sunbeams,
Point their shafts against my care,
  Heard them shattering my dreams.

All the house their carol shook,
  To my soul their joy gave wing,
Gave my sight an upward look,
  Opened it like flowers in spring ;

Into perfume seemed to burst,
  And to offer up my heart,
Changing into best my worst,
  Into comfort every smart.

Lightly then my straining mind
  Threw its ladder to the sky,
Upward ran the morn to find,
  See its surf run freshening by.

Gladness was the friend I found,
  Sense of something clear and still ;
As the earth in light is drowned,
  And in space the highest hill.

All my prose to song sublimed,
　All my waiting to this smile,
Hung, without a flutter, rhymed
　In the heaven's perfect style.

Did my life indeed ascend,
　Or some life sink down to me?
All I know, it was my Friend:
　Name it? shape it?　Let that be.

METHOD

CENTRAL axis, pole of pole,
Central ark and goal of goal,
Worship, to whose sovereign end
All the spirit's uses tend.
Taught of her high mystery,
Perfect will the man-child be.
Not with sorrow, not with moan
Comes the soul unto her own;
Not with sounding steps of thunder,
Not with flaming looks of fire,
But with calm delight and wonder,
Simple hope and sweet desire.
Then, through all the motions stealing

METHOD

Of the manifold existence,
Ever lifting, soothing, healing,
Love attunes each thought and feeling
Unto patience and persistence.

Thomas Wentworth Higginson

THE THINGS I MISS

An easy thing, O Power Divine,
To thank Thee for these gifts of Thine!
For summer's sunshine, winter's snow,
For hearts that kindle, thoughts that glow.
But when shall I attain to this, —
To thank Thee for the things I miss?

For all young Fancy's early gleams,
The dreamed-of joys that still are dreams,
Hopes unfulfilled, and pleasures known
Through others' fortunes, not my own,
And blessings seen that are not given,
And never will be, this side heaven.

Had I too shared the joys I see,
Would there have been a heaven for me?
Could I have felt Thy presence near,
Had I possessed what I held dear?
My deepest fortune, highest bliss,
Have grown perchance from things I miss.

Sometimes there comes an hour of calm;
Grief turns to blessing, pain to balm;
A Power that works above my will
Still leads me onward, upward still.
And then my heart attains to this, —
To thank Thee for the things I miss.

HEIRS OF TIME

FROM street and square, from hill and glen
Of this vast world beyond my door,
I hear the tread of marching men,
The patient armies of the poor.

The halo of the city's lamps
Hangs, a vast torchlight, in the air;
I watch it through the evening damps:
The masters of the world are there.

Not ermine-clad or clothed in state,
Their title-deeds not yet made plain;
But waking early, toiling late,
The heirs of all the earth remain.

Some day, by laws as fixed and fair
As guide the planets in their sweep,

The children of each outcast heir
The harvest-fruits of time shall reap.

The peasant brain shall yet be wise,
The untamed pulse grow calm and still;
The blind shall see, the lowly rise,
And work in peace Time's wondrous will.

Some day, without a trumpet's call,
This news will o'er the world be blown:
"The heritage comes back to all!
The myriad monarchs take their own!"

A JAR OF ROSE–LEAVES

MYRIAD roses fade unheeded,
Yet no note of grief is needed;
When the ruder breezes tear them,
Sung or songless, we can spare them.
But the choicest petals are
Shrined in some deep Orient jar,
Rich without and sweet within,
Where we cast the rose-leaves in

Life has jars of costlier price
Framed to hold our memories.

There we treasure baby smiles,
Boyish exploits, girlish wiles,
All that made our early days
Sweeter than these trodden ways
Where the Fates our fortunes spin :
Memory, toss the rose-leaves in !

What the jar holds, that shall stay ;
Time steals all the rest away.
Cast in love's first stolen word,
Bliss when uttered, bliss when heard ;
Maiden's looks of shy surprise ;
Glances from a hero's eyes ;
Palms we risked our souls to win :
Memory, fling the rose-leaves in !

Now more sombre and more slow
Let the incantation grow !
Cast in shreds of rapture brief,
Subtle links 'twixt hope and grief ;
Vagrant fancy's dangerous toys ;
Covert dreams, narcotic joys
Flavored with the taste of sin :
Memory, pour the rose-leaves in !

Quit that borderland of pain !
Cast in thoughts of nobler vein,

Magic gifts of human breath,
Mysteries of birth and death.
What if all this web of change
But prepare for scenes more strange ;
If to die be to begin ?
Memory, heap the rose-leaves in !

ODE TO A BUTTERFLY

THOU spark of life that wavest wings of gold,
Thou songless wanderer 'mid the songful birds,
With Nature's secrets in thy tints unrolled
Through gorgeous cipher, past the reach of words,
    Yet dear to every child
    In glad pursuit beguiled,
Living his unspoiled days 'mid flowers and flocks
    and herds !

Thou wingèd blossom, liberated thing,
What secret tie binds thee to other flowers,
Still held within the garden's fostering ?
Will they too soar with the completed hours,
    Take flight, and be like thee
    Irrevocably free,
Hovering at will o'er their parental bowers ?

Or is thy lustre drawn from heavenly hues, —
A sumptuous drifting fragment of the sky,
Caught when the sunset its last glance imbues
With sudden splendor, and the treetops high
    Grasp that swift blazonry,
    Then lend those tints to thee,
On thee to float a few short hours, and die?

Birds have their nests; they rear their eager
    young,
And flit on errands all the livelong day;
Each fieldmouse keeps the homestead whence it
    sprung;
But thou art Nature's freeman, — free to stray
    Unfettered through the wood,
    Sucking thine airy food,
The sweetness spiced on every blossomed spray.

The garden one wide banquet spreads for thee,
O daintiest reveller of the joyous earth!
One drop of honey gives satiety;
A second draught would drug thee past all mirth.
    Thy feast no orgy shows;
    Thy calm eyes never close,
Thou soberest sprite to which the sun gives birth.

And yet the soul of man upon thy wings
Forever soars in aspiration ; thou
His emblem of the new career that springs
When death's arrest bids all his spirit bow.
    He seeks his hope in thee
    Of immortality.
Symbol of life, me with such faith endow !

George Shepard Burleigh

DARE AND KNOW

THE truths we cannot win are fruit forbidden,
That knowledge only is, by proof not ours,
Which lies beyond the measure of our powers:
Not by God's grudging are our natures chidden,
His hidden things for daring search are hidden:
The cloudy darkness that around him lowers
Burns only with his glory, and the dowers
Of Hero-hearts who have gone up and ridden
The storm like eagles!   If the lightning singe
The intrepid wing, 't is but the burning kiss
Of Victory in Espousal, — the keen bliss
Whose rapturous thrill might make the coward
        cringe!
He who aloft on Rood-nails hung our crown
Smiles when with bleeding hands we climb and
        pluck it down!

THE IDEAL WINS

THOUGH hunger sharpens in the dream of food,
And thirst burns fiercer for the visioned brook,

Our souls are drawn the way our longings look,
And our ideal good is actual good.
The heavens we win are more than we pursued ;
For the great Dream has cheapened the small
      nook
That once for all the rounded world we took,
And our sect sinks in boundless Brotherhood.
By noble climbing, though the heavens recede,
Broader expands the horizon's girdling wall ;
Through misty doubts we reach the sunnier creed,
And, nearer heaven, see earth a fairer ball ;
And souls that soar beyond their simple need,
To grasp the highest, are made free of all !

IMMANUEL

THE Law which spheres the hugest sun
    That blazes in the deeps of blue,
And binds unnumbered worlds in one,
    So rounds the tiniest drop of dew.

The God who sowed the midnight gloom
    With stars that blossom evermore,
Still lights the lowliest lily-bloom
    That nestles by the cottage door.

IMMANUEL

An atom of the self-same fire
    That burned in Zoroaster's soul,
Kindles the humblest heart's desire,
    And beacons our eternal goal.

What Jesus felt, what Moses saw
    On Sinai, on Gennesaret,
Love's boundless glow, the lightning Law,
    Our hearts have known, our vision met.

For God in every nature folds
    The perfect future of its kind;
The eternal love thy bosom holds,
    And thrills thy thought the Eternal Mind.

Oh, not in overweening pride,
    But calm in holy trust alone,
Put every alien law aside,
    And walk serenely by thy own.

Cathayan clogs, Judean creeds,
    Deform and fetter limb and soul;
Life only from within proceeds,
    Evolving one harmonious whole.

The heart, self-centred, that alone
Obeys what God within it bids,
Holds firmly its inviolate throne
As Andes and the Pyramids.

OUR BIRTHRIGHT

As children of the Infinite Soul
Our Birthright is the boundless whole,
Won truth by truth while endless ages roll.

Swift Fancy's wing would flag in flight
To reach the depth, the breadth, and height
Of the vast wealth that waits our growing sight:

High truths which have not yet been dreamed,
Realities of all that seemed
Best in the best of what we hoped and deemed:

Such freedom under natural law
As not the fabled Eden saw,
So large and calm, and full of blissful awe:

And love that cannot fail to flow,
Warm as the sun and white as snow,
Through flesh and soul that sweet as lilies grow:

OUR BIRTHRIGHT

With knowledge that on sea and land
And air shall lay familiar hand,
And weigh the star-dust on creation's strand;

And wisdom ever more divine,
Of clustered knowledge the red wine,
Which holds the world dissolved and crystalline.

Peace over all in skyey calm
Shall weave her olive with the palm
Of victory, and steep the earth in balm.

A thousand years the soul shall climb
To guess what more of wealth sublime
Waits for a conqueror in the depths of time.

The fiends who guard it, hunger-gnawed,
Are Doubt and Fear and ancient Fraud,
And grey old Use by whom the world is awed.

But heralds of the better day
Beckon us on, and point the way,
Where earnest seeking never goes astray.

No peril daunts the Brave; he speeds
Across the wreck of older creeds,
And crownless gods cast down among the weeds.

Doubt dies beneath his lifted spear,
Fraud slinks away with breathless Fear,
And grey old Use shrieks in his heedless ear.

Wide gape these parasites aghast
As in the temples of the Past
He sets the ark of living Godhood fast;

And hollow gods, to whom they pledge
Libations on their altar-ledge,
Fall shattered down to bite the grunsel's edge.

Well may ye deem that pain and loss
Will haunt his walks, and murder toss
On him the boding shadow of her cross.

But loss and pain will wear away
The thick opacity of clay,
And the cross lift him to the zone of day!

Far-seeking his imperial goal,
No fate can rob the earnest soul
Of his great birthright in the boundless whole!

William Henry Furness

THE SOUL

WHAT is this that stirs within,
Loving goodness, hating sin,
Always craving to be blest,
Finding here below no rest?

Nought that charms the ear or eye
Can its hunger satisfy;
Active, restless, it would pierce
Through the outward universe.

What is it? and whither? whence?
This unsleeping, secret sense,
Longing for its rest and food
In some hidden, untried good?

'T is the soul!   Mysterious name!
Him it seeks from whom it came;
It would, Mighty God, like thee,
Holy, holy, holy be!

EVENING

Slowly by thy hand unfurled,
Down around the weary world
Falls the darkness.   Oh, how still
Is the working of thy will!

Mighty Maker!   Here am I,
Work in me as silently;
Veil the day's distracting sights,
Show me heaven's eternal lights.

From the darkened sky come forth
Countless stars. A wondrous birth!
So may gleams of glory dart
From this dim abyss, my heart.

Living worlds to view be brought
In the boundless realms of thought;
High and infinite desires,
Flashing like those upper fires.

Holy Truth, Eternal Right,
Let them break upon my sight;

Let them shine, serene and still,
And with light my being fill.

Thou, who dwellest there, I know,
Dwellest here within me, too ;
May the perfect love of God,
Here, as there, be shed abroad.

Let my soul attunèd be
To the heavenly harmony,
Which, beyond the power of sound,
Fills the Universe around.

Samuel Johnson

FOR DIVINE STRENGTH

FATHER, in thy mysterious presence kneeling,
  Fain would our souls feel all thy kindling love ;
For we are weak, and need some deep revealing
  Of trust, and strength, and calmness from above.

Lord, we have wandered far through doubt and
      sorrow,
  And thou hast made each step an onward one ;
And we will ever trust each unknown morrow, —
  Thou wilt sustain us till its work is done.

In the heart's depths a peace serene and holy
  Abides ; and when pain seems to have its will,
Or we despair, O may that peace rise slowly,
  Stronger than agony, and we be still !

Now, Father, now, in thy dear presence kneeling,
  Our spirits yearn to feel thy kindling love ;
Now make us strong, we need thy deep revealing
  Of trust, and strength, and calmness from above.

INSPIRATION

LIFE of Ages, richly poured,
  Love of God, unspent and free,
Flowing in the prophet's word
  And the people's liberty!

Never was to chosen race
  That unstinted tide confined;
Thine is every time and place,
  Fountain sweet of heart and mind!

Secret of the morning stars,
  Motion of the oldest hours,
Pledge through elemental wars
  Of the coming spirit's powers!

Rolling planet, flaming sun,
  Stand in nobler man complete;
Prescient laws thine errands run,
  Frame the shrine for Godhead meet.

Homeward led, the wondering eye
  Upward yearned in joy or awe,

Found the love that waited nigh,
  Guidance of thy guardian law.

In the touch of earth it thrilled;
  Down from mystic skies it burned;
Right obeyed and passion stilled
  Its eternal gladness earned.

Breathing in the thinker's creed,
  Pulsing in the hero's blood,
Nerving simplest thought and deed,
  Freshening time with truth and good,

Consecrating art and song,
  Holy book and pilgrim track,
Hurling floods of tyrant wrong
  From the sacred limits back, —

Life of Ages, richly poured,
  Love of God, unspent and free,
Flow still in the Prophet's word
  And the People's liberty!

Samuel Longfellow

LOOKING UNTO GOD

"Who sees God's hand in all things, and all things in God's
hand."

I LOOK to thee in every need,
  And never look in vain ;
I feel thy touch, Eternal Love !
  And all is well again.
The thought of thee is mightier far
Than sin and pain and sorrow are.

Discouraged in the work of life,
  Disheartened by its load,
Shamed by its failures or its fears,
  I sink beside the road, —
But let me only think of thee,
And then new heart springs up in me.

Thy calmness bends serene above,
  My restlessness to still ;

Around me flows thy quickening life
   To nerve my faltering will ;
Thy presence fills my solitude,
Thy providence turns all to good.

Embosomed deep in thy dear love,
   Held in thy law, I stand ;
Thy hand in all things I behold,
   And all things in thy hand ;
Thou leadest me by unsought ways,
And turn'st my mourning into praise.

THE CHURCH UNIVERSAL

ONE holy church of God appears
   Through every age and race,
Unwasted by the lapse of years,
   Unchanged by changing place.

From oldest time, on farthest shores,
   Beneath the pine or palm,
One Unseen Presence she adores
   With silence or with psalm.

Her priests are all God's faithful sons,
   To serve the world raised up ;

The pure in heart her baptized ones,
    Love her communion-cup.

The truth is her prophetic gift,
    The soul her sacred page;
And feet on mercy's errands swift
    Do make her pilgrimage.

O living Church! thine errand speed,
    Fulfil thy work sublime;
With bread of life earth's hunger feed,
    Redeem the evil time!

Eliza Scudder

THE LOVE OF GOD

Thou Grace Divine, encircling all,
  A soundless, shoreless sea
Wherein at last our souls must fall! —
  O Love of God most free!

When over dizzy heights we go,
  One soft hand blinds our eyes,
The other leads us, safe and slow, —
  O Love of God most wise!

And though we turn us from Thy face,
  And wander wide and long,
Thou hold'st us still in Thine embrace, —
  O Love of God most strong!

The saddened heart, the restless soul,
  The toil-worn frame and mind,
Alike confess Thy sweet control, —
  O Love of God most kind!

But not alone Thy care we claim,
　　Our wayward steps to win:
We know Thee by a dearer name, —
　　O Love of God within!

And filled and quickened by Thy breath,
　　Our souls are strong and free
To rise o'er sin and fear and death,
　　O Love of God, to Thee!

WHOM BUT THEE

FROM past regret and present faithlessness,
From the deep shadow of foreseen distress,
And from the nameless weariness that grows
As life's long day seems wearing to its close;

Thou Life within my life, than self more near!
Thou veilèd Presence infinitely clear!
From all illusive shows of sense I flee
To find my centre and my rest in Thee.

Below all depths Thy saving mercy lies,
Through thickest glooms I see Thy Light arise;
Above the highest heavens Thou art not found
More surely than within this earthly round.

215

Take part with me against these doubts that rise
And seek to throne Thee far in distant skies !
Take part with me against this self that dares
Assume the burden of these sins and cares !

How shall I call Thee who art always here,
How shall I praise Thee who art still most dear,
What may I give Thee save what Thou hast given,
And whom but Thee have I in earth or heaven?

TRUTH

THOU long disowned, reviled, opprest,
  Strange friend of human kind,
Seeking through weary years a rest
  Within our heart to find.

How late thy bright and awful brow
  Breaks through these clouds of sin !
Hail, Truth Divine ! we know thee now,
  Angel of God, come in !

Come, though with purifying fire
  And desolating sword,
Thou of all nations the desire,
  Earth waits Thy cleansing word.

Struck by the lightning of Thy glance
   Let old oppressions die!
Before Thy cloudless countenance
   Let fear and falsehood fly!

Anoint our eyes with healing grace
   To see as ne'er before
Our Father, in our brother's face,
   Our Master, in his poor.

Flood our dark life with golden day!
   Convince, subdue, enthrall!
Then to a mightier yield Thy sway,
   And Love be all in all!

NO MORE SEA

LIFE of our life, and Light of all our seeing,
   How shall we rest on any hope but Thee?
What time our souls, to Thee for refuge fleeing,
   Long for the home where there is no more sea?

For still this sea of life, with endless wailing,
   Dashes above our heads its blinding spray,
And vanquished hearts, sick with remorse and failing,
   Moan like the waves at set of autumn day.

And ever round us swells the insatiate ocean
  Of sin and doubt that lures us to our grave;
When its wild billows, with their mad commotion,
  Would sweep us down — then only Thou canst
    save.

And deep and dark the fearful gloom unlighted
  Of that untried and all-surrounding sea,
On whose bleak shore arriving lone, benighted,
  We fall and lose ourselves at last — in Thee.

Yea! in Thy life our little lives are ended,
  Into Thy depths our trembling spirits fall;
In Thee enfolded, gathered, comprehended,
  As holds the sea her waves — Thou hold'st us
    all!

THANKSGIVING

"We bless Thee . . . for the means of grace and for the hope
of glory."

For the rapt stillness of the place
  Where sacred song and ordered prayer
Wait the unveiling of Thy face,
  And seek Thy angels' joys to share;

For souls won o'er to truth and right,
   For wisdom dropping as the dew,
For Thy great Word in lines of light,
   Made visible to mortal view;

For gladness of the summer morning,
   For fair faint twilight's lingering ray,
For forest's and for field's adorning,
   And the wild ocean's ceaseless play;

For flowers unsought, in desert places
   Flashing enchantment on the sight;
For radiance on familiar faces
   As they passed upward into light;

For blessings of the fruitful season,
   For work and rest, for friends and home,
For the great gifts of thought and reason, —
   To praise and bless Thee, Lord, we come.

Yes, and for weeping and for wailing,
   For bitter hail and blighting frost,
For high hopes on the low earth trailing,
   For sweet joys missed, for pure aims crost;

For lonely toil and tribulation,
   And e'en for hidings of Thy face, —

For these Thy heralds of salvation,
    Thy means and messengers of grace.

With joy supreme, with faith unbroken,
    With worship passing thought or speech,
Of Thy dear love we hail each token,
    And give Thee humble thanks for each.

For o'er our struggling and our sighing,
    Now quenched in mist, now glimmering far
Above our living and our dying,
    Hangs high in Heaven one beckoning star.

And when we gather up the story
    Of all Thy mercies flowing free,
Crown of them all, that hope of glory,
    Of growing ever nearer Thee.

VESPER HYMN

THE day is done, the weary day of thought and
        toil is past,
Soft falls the twilight cool and gray on the tired
        earth at last :

By wisest teachers wearied, by gentlest friends op-
      prest,
In Thee alone the soul, outworn, refreshment finds
      and rest.

Bend, gracious Spirit, from above, like these o'er-
      arching skies,
And to Thy firmament of love lift up these long-
      ing eyes;
And, folded by Thy sheltering Hand, in refuge
      still and deep,
Let blessed thoughts from Thee descend, as drop
      the dews of sleep.

And when refreshed the soul once more puts on
      new life and power;
Oh, let Thine image, Lord, alone, gild the first
      waking hour!
Let that dear Presence dawn and glow, fairer than
      morn's first ray,
And Thy pure radiance overflow the splendor of
      the day.

So in the hastening evening, so in the coming morn,
When deeper slumber shall be given, and fresher
      life be born,

Shine out, true Light! to guide my way amid that
    deepening gloom,
And rise, O Morning Star, the first that dayspring
    to illume!

I cannot dread the darkness where Thou wilt
    watch o'er me,
Nor smile to greet the sunrise unless Thy smile I
    see;
Creator, Saviour, Comforter! on Thee my soul is
    cast;
At morn, at night, in earth, in heaven, be Thou
    my First and Last!

THE QUEST

"Whither shall I go from Thy spirit? or whither shall I flee
from Thy presence?"

I CANNOT find Thee! Still on restless pinion
  My spirit beats the void where Thou dost dwell;
I wander lost through all Thy vast dominion,
  And shrink beneath Thy Light ineffable.

I cannot find Thee! E'en when most adoring
  Before Thy throne I bend in lowliest prayer;

Beyond these bounds of thought, my thought up-
    soaring,
  From farthest quest comes back; Thou art not
    there.

Yet high above the limits of my seeing,
  And folded far within the inmost heart,
And deep below the deeps of conscious being,
  Thy splendor shineth; there, O God, Thou art.

I cannot lose Thee! Still in Thee abiding
  The end is clear, how wide soe'er I roam;
The Hand that holds the worlds my steps is guid-
    ing,
  And I must rest at last, in Thee, my home.

Helen Hunt Jackson

LOVE'S FULFILLING

O LOVE is weak
Which counts the answers and the gains,
Weighs all the losses and the pains,
And eagerly each fond word drains
    A joy to seek.

When Love is strong,
It never tarries to take heed,
Or know if its return exceed
Its gifts ; in its sweet haste no greed,
    No strifes belong.

It hardly asks
If it be loved at all ; to take
So barren seems, when it can make
Such bliss, for the belovèd sake,
    Of bitter tasks.

Its ecstasy
Could find hard death so beauteous,
It sees through tears how Christ loved us,
And speaks, in saying " I love thus,"
    No blasphemy.

So much we miss
If love is weak, so much we gain
If love is strong, God thinks no pain
Too sharp or lasting to ordain
    To teach us this.

" NOT AS I WILL "

BLINDFOLDED and alone I stand
With unknown thresholds on each hand;
The darkness deepens as I grope,
Afraid to fear, afraid to hope:
Yet this one thing I learn to know
Each day more surely as I go,
That doors are opened, ways are made,
Burdens are lifted or are laid,
By some great law unseen and still,
Unfathomed purpose to fulfil,
    " Not as I will."

Blindfolded and alone I wait ;
Loss seems too bitter, gain too late ;
Too heavy burdens in the load
And too few helpers on the road ;
And joy is weak and grief is strong,
And years and days so long, so long :
Yet this one thing I learn to know
Each day more surely as I go,
That I am glad the good and ill
By changeless law are ordered still,
    " Not as I will."

" Not as I will : " the sound grows sweet
Each time my lips the words repeat.
" Not as I will : " the darkness feels
More safe than light when this thought steals
Like whispered voice to calm and bless
All unrest and all loneliness.
" Not as I will," because the One
Who loved us first and best has gone
Before us on the road, and still
For us must all his love fulfil,
    " Not as we will."

SPINNING

LIKE a blind spinner in the sun,
     I tread my days;
I know that all the threads will run
     Appointed ways;
I know each day will bring its task;
And, being blind, no more I ask.

I do not know the use or name
     Of that I spin;
I only know that some one came,
     And laid within
My hand the thread, and said, "Since you
Are blind, but one thing you can do."

Sometimes the threads so rough and fast
     And tangled fly,
I know wild storms are sweeping past,
     And fear that I
Shall fall, but dare not try to find
A safer place, since I am blind.

I know not why, but I am sure
            That tint and place,
In some great fabric to endure
            Past time and race,
My threads will have ; so from the first,
Though blind, I never felt accurst.

I think, perhaps, this trust has sprung
            From one short word
Said over me when I was young, —
            So young, I heard
It, knowing not that God's name signed
My brow, and sealed me his, though blind.

But whether this be seal or sign
            Within, without,
It matters not.   The bond divine
            I never doubt.
I know he set me here, and still,
And glad, and blind, I wait his will ;

But listen, listen, day by day,
            To hear their tread
Who bear the finished web away,
            And cut the thread,
And bring God's message in the sun,
" Thou poor blind spinner, work is done."

HYMN

I CANNOT think but God must know
About the thing I long for so;
I know He is so good, so kind,
I cannot think but He will find
Some way to help, some way to show
Me to the thing I long for so.

I stretch my hand — it lies so near:
It looks so sweet, it looks so dear.
" Dear Lord," I pray, " Oh let me know
If it is wrong to want it so ? "
He only smiles, — He does not speak:
My heart grows weaker and more weak,
With looking at the thing so dear,
Which lies so far, and yet so near.

Now, Lord, I leave at Thy loved feet
This thing which looks so near, so sweet;
I will not seek, I will not long, —
I almost fear I have been wrong.

229

I 'll go, and work the harder, Lord,
And wait till by some loud, clear word
Thou callest me to Thy loved feet,
To take this thing so dear, so sweet.

THE LOVE OF GOD

LIKE a cradle rocking, rocking,
   Silent, peaceful, to and fro,
Like a mother's sweet looks dropping
   On the little face below,
Hangs the green earth, swinging, turning,
   Jarless, noiseless, safe, and slow;
Falls the light of God's face bending
   Down and watching us below.

And as feeble babes that suffer,
   Toss, and cry, and will not rest,
Are the ones the tender mother
   Holds the closest, loves the best, —
So when we are weak and wretched,
   By our sins weighed down, distressed,
Then it is that God's great patience
   Holds us closest, loves us best.

Edward Rowland Sill

LIFE

FORENOON and afternoon and night, — Forenoon,
And afternoon, and night, — Forenoon, and —
    what!
The empty song repeats itself.   No more?
Yes, that is Life : make this forenoon sublime,
This afternoon a psalm, this night a prayer,
And Time is conquered, and thy crown is won.

THE FUTURE

WHAT may we take into the vast Forever?
      That marble door
Admits no fruit of all our long endeavor,
       No fame-wreathed crown we wore,
       No garnered lore.

What can we bear beyond the unknown portal?
       No gold, no gains

Of all our toiling : in the life immortal
No hoarded wealth remains,
No gilds, nor stains.

Naked from out that far abyss behind us
We entered here :
No word came with our coming, to remind us
What wondrous world was near,
No hope, no fear.

Into the silent, starless Night before us,
Naked we glide :
No hand has mapped the constellations o'er
us,
No comrade at our side,
No chart, no guide.

Yet fearless toward that midnight, black and
hollow,
Our footsteps fare :
The beckoning of a Father's hand we fol-
low —
His love alone is there,
No curse, no care.

A PRAYER

_____

A PRAYER

O GOD, our Father, if we had but truth!
    Lost truth — which thou perchance
Didst let man lose, lest all his wayward youth
    He waste in song and dance;
That he might gain, in searching, mightier powers,
For manlier use in those foreshadowed hours.

If blindly groping, he shall oft mistake,
    And follow twinkling motes
Thinking them stars, and the one voice forsake
    Of Wisdom for the notes
Which mocking Beauty utters here and there,
Thou surely wilt forgive him, and forbear!

Oh love us, for we love thee, Maker — God!
    And would creep near thy hand,
And call thee " Father, Father," from the sod
    Where by our graves we stand,
And pray to touch, fearless of scorn or blame,
The garment's hem, which Truth and Good we
        name.

WIEGENLIED

Be still and sleep, my soul!
  Now gentle-footed Night
In softly shadowed stole
  Holds all the day from sight.

Why shouldst thou lie and stare
  Against the dark, and toss,
And live again thy care,
  Thine agony and loss?

'T was given thee to live,
  And thou hast lived it all;
Let that suffice, nor give
  One thought what may befall.

Thou hast no need to wake,
  Thou art no sentinel;
Love all the care will take,
  And Wisdom watcheth well.

Weep not, think not, but rest!
  The stars in silence roll;
On the world's mother-breast,
  Be still and sleep, my soul!

FORCE

THE stars know a secret
  They do not tell;
And morn brings a message
  Hidden well.

There's a blush on the apple,
  A tint on the wing,
And the bright wind whistles,
  And the pulses sting.

Perish dark memories!
  There's light ahead;
This world's for the living;
  Not for the dead.

In the shining city,
  On the loud pave,
The life-tide is running,
  Like a leading wave.

235

How the stream quickens,
   As noon draws near,
No room for loiterers,
   No time for fear.

Out on the farm lands
   Earth smiles as well;
Gold-crusted grain-fields,
   With sweet, warm smell;

Whir of the reaper,
   Like a giant bee;
Like a Titan cricket,
   Thrilling with glee.

On mart and meadow,
   Pavement or plain;
On azure mountain,
   Or azure main —

Heaven bends in blessing;
   Lost is but won;
Goes the good rain-cloud,
   Comes the good sun!

Only babes whimper,
   And sick men wail,

And faint hearts and feeble hearts
  And weaklings fail.

Down the great currents
  Let the boat swing ;
There was never winter
  But brought the spring.

TRANQUILLITY

WEARY, and marred with care and pain
And bruising days, the human brain
Draws wounded inward, — it might be
Some delicate creature of the sea,
That, shuddering, shrinks its lucent dome,
And coils its azure tendrils home,
And folds its filmy curtains tight
At jarring contact, e'er so light ;
But let it float away all free,
And feel the buoyant, supple sea
Among its tinted streamers swell,
Again it spreads its gauzy wings,
And, waving its wan fringes, swings
With rhythmic pulse its crystal bell.

237

So let the mind, with care o'erwrought,
Float down the tranquil tides of thought:
Calm visions of unending years
Beyond this little moment's fears;
Of boundless regions far from where
The girdle of the azure air
Binds to the earth the prisoned mind.
Set free the fancy, let it find
Beyond our world a vaster place
To thrill and vibrate out through space, —
As some auroral banner streams
Up through the night in pulsing gleams,
And floats and flashes o'er our dreams;
There let the whirling planet fall
Down — down, till but a glimmering ball,
A misty star: and dwindled so,
There is no room for care, or woe,
Or wish, apart from that one Will
That doth the worlds with music fill.

PEACE

'T is not in seeking,
'T is not in endless striving,
Thy quest is found:

PEACE

Be still and listen ;
Be still and drink the quiet
  Of all around.

Not for thy crying,
Not for thy loud beseeching,
  Will peace draw near :
Rest with palms folded ;
Rest with thine eyelids fallen —
  Lo ! peace is here.

Julia Ward Howe

STANZAS

Of the heaven is generation:
Fruition in the deep earth lies:
And where the twain have broadest blending,
The stateliest growths of life arise.

Set, then, thy root in earth more firmly:
Raise thy head erect and free:
And spread thy loving arms so widely,
That heaven and earth shall meet in thee.

WARNING

Power, reft of aspiration;
Passion, lacking inspiration;
Leisure, not of contemplation.

Thus shall danger overcome thee,
Fretted luxury consume thee,
All divineness vanish from thee.

240

Be a man, and be one wholly;
Keep one great love, purely, solely,
Till it make thy nature holy;

That thy way be paved in whiteness,
That thy heart may beat in lightness,
That thy being end in brightness.

THE PRICE OF THE DIVINA COMMEDIA

GIVE, — you need not see the face,
But the garment hangeth bare;
And the hand is gaunt and spare
That enforces Christian grace.

Many ages will not bring
Such a point as this to sight,
That the world should so requite
Master heart and matchless string.

Wonder at the well-born feet
Fretting in the flinty road.
Hath this virtue no abode?
Hath this sorrow no retreat?

See, beneath the hood of grief,
Muffled bays engird the brow.
Fame shall yield her topmost bough
Ere that laurel moult a leaf.

Give: it is no idle hand
That extends an asking palm,
Tracing yet the loftiest psalm
By the heart of Nature spanned.

In the antechamber long
Did he patient hearing crave:
Smiles and splendors crown the slave,
While the patriot suffers wrong.

Could the mighty audience deign,
Meeting once the inspired gaze,
They should ransom all their days
With the beauty of his strain.

With a spasm in his breast,
With a consummate love alone,
All his human blessings gone,
Doth he wander, void of rest.

Not a coin within his purse,
Not a crust to help his way,

Making yet a Judgment Day
With his power to bless and curse.

Give; but ask what he has given:
That Posterity shall tell, —
All the majesty of Hell;
Half the ecstasy of Heaven.

THE HOUSE OF REST

I WILL build a house of rest,
Square the corners every one:
At each angle on his breast
Shall a cherub take the sun;
Rising, risen, sinking, down,
Weaving day's unequal crown.

In the chambers, light as air,
Shall responsive footsteps fall:
Brother, sister, art thou there?
Hush! we need not jar nor call;
Need not turn to seek the face
Shut in rapture's hiding-place.

Heavy load and mocking care
Shall from back and bosom part;

Thought shall reach the thrill of prayer,
Patience plan the dome of art.
None shall praise or merit claim,
Not a joy be called by name.

With a free, unmeasured tread
Shall we pace the cloisters through:
Rest, enfranchised, like the Dead;
Rest till Love be born anew.
Weary Thought shall take his time,
Free of task-work, loosed from rhyme.

No reproof shall grieve or chill;
Every sin doth stand confest;
None need murmur, " This was ill: "
Therefore do they grant us rest;
Contemplation making whole
Every ruin of the soul.

Pictures shall as softly look
As in distance shows delight;
Slowly shall each saintly book
Turn its pages in our sight;
Not the study's wealth confuse,
Urging zeal to pale abuse.

THE HOUSE OF REST

Children through the windows peep,
Not reproachful, though our own;
Hushed the parent passion deep,
And the household's eager tone.
One above, divine and true,
Makes us children like to you.

Measured bread shall build us up
At the hospitable board;
In Contentment's golden cup
Is the guileless liquor poured.
May the beggar pledge the king
In that spirit gathering.

Oh! my house is far away;
Yet it sometimes shuts me in.
Imperfection mars each day
While the perfect works begin.
In the house of labor best
Can I build the house of rest.

Ednah Dow Cheney

PRAYER

At first I prayed for sight;
  Could I but see the way,
How gladly would I walk
  To everlasting day.
I asked the world's deep law
  Before my eyes to ope,
And let me see my prayers fulfilled,
  And realized, my hope;
But God was kinder than my prayer,
  And mystery veiled me everywhere.

And next I prayed for strength
  That I might tread the road,
With firm unfaltering pace,
  To heaven's serene abode.
That I might never know
  A faltering, failing heart;
But manfully go on
  And reach the highest part.

But God was kinder than my prayer,
   And weakness checked me everywhere.

And then I asked for faith ;
   Could I but trust my God,
I 'd live in heavenly peace
   Though foes were all abroad.
His light thus shining round,
   No faltering should I know ;
And faith in heaven above
   Would make a heaven below ;
But God was kinder than my prayer,
   And doubts beset me everywhere.

And now I pray for love,
   Deep love to God and man ;
A love that will not fail,
   However dark his plan ;
That sees all life in Him,
   Rejoicing in his power ;
And faithful, though the darkest clouds
   Of gloom and doubt may lower.
And God was kinder than my prayer,
   Love filled and blessed me everywhere.

WAITING HELP

The question was asked, "To Whom do Free Religionists pray?"
The reply was, "To Whomsoever they believe will help them."

WHATE'ER the Name, whate'er the Power,
That helped me in my bitter hour,
I know there came a Strength not mine,
A peace not earthly, but Divine.

That peace, that strength, I know it waits
For every heart that opes its gates,
To let the Gracious Presence in;
And with its help new life begin.

So waits the morning in the skies,
Until the sleeper opes his eyes;
So breaks the Sea on every shore,
The sick and weary to restore.

Each lovely flower, each busy bee,
Says, " Only come, I 'll give to thee;"
The North Star waited, æons back,
To guide the slave on freedom's track.

Each hero soul, each martyr heart,
In thy deep pain has borne its part;
And every triumph in the skies
Has helped my unfledged soul to rise.

The Over-soul, the All, the Law,
The God whom mortal eyes ne'er saw,
And yet whose presence all things knew,
'T was that helped me and will help you.

"I SHALL BE SATISFIED WHEN I AWAKE WITH THY LIKENESS"

" WAKEN in Thy likeness," meet Thee face to face,
   Know the sweet unfoldings of Thy perfect love,
All the wondrous meaning of Thy wisdom trace,
   All the perfect justice of Thine order prove.

" Waken in Thy likeness," be what Thou hast
      willed,
   Know the sweet communion hearts can meet in
      Thee,
All earth's restless passions, all its longings
      stilled,
   All times blended in Eternity.

" Waken in Thy likeness," knowing all Thy truth,
    Loving all Thy children, living in Thy breath,
Blossoming forever in the joy of youth.
    Break thy peaceful slumber, waken me, oh
        Death !

John Burroughs

WAITING

Serene, I fold my hands and wait,
   Nor care for wind, or tide, or sea;
I rave no more 'gainst Time or Fate,
   For lo! my own shall come to me.

I stay my haste, I make delays,
   For what avails this eager pace?
I stand amid the eternal ways,
   And what is mine shall know my face.

Asleep, awake, by night or day,
   The friends I seek are seeking me;
No wind can drive my bark astray,
   Nor change the tide of destiny.

What matter if I stand alone?
   I wait with joy the coming years;
My heart shall reap where it hath sown,
   And garner up its fruit of tears.

The waters know their own, and draw
  The brook that springs in yonder height;
So flows the good with equal law
  Unto the soul of pure delight.

The stars come nightly to the sky;
  The tidal wave unto the sea;
Nor time, nor space, nor deep, nor high,
  Can keep my own away from me.

GOLDEN CROWN SPARROW OF ALASKA

Oh, minstrel of these borean hills,
  Where twilight hours are long,
I would my boyhood's fragrant days
  Had known thy plaintive song;

Had known thy vest of ashen gray,
  Thy coat of drab and brown,
The bands of jet upon thy head
  That clasp thy golden crown.

We heard thee in the cold White Pass,
  Where cloud and mountain meet,

Again where Muir's glacier shone
   Far spread beneath our feet.

I bask me now on emerald heights
   To catch thy faintest strain,
But cannot tell if in thy lay
   Be more of joy or pain.

Far off behold the snow-white peaks
   Athwart the sea's blue-shade ;
Anear there rise green Kadiak hills,
   Wherein thy nest is made.

I hear the wild bee's mellow chord,
   In airs that swim above ;
The lesser hermit tunes his flute
   To solitude and love.

But thou, sweet singer of the wild,
   I give more heed to thee ;
Thy wistful note of fond regret
   Strikes deeper chords in me.

Farewell, dear bird ! I turn my face
   To other skies than thine —
A thousand leagues of land and sea
   Between thy home and mine.

Franklin Benjamin Sanborn

ANATHEMATA

"O maiden! come into port bravely, or sail with God the seas."

WITH joys unknown, with sadness unconfessed,
The generous heart accepts the passing year,
Finds duties dear, and labor sweet as rest,
And for itself knows neither care nor fear.
Fresh as the morning, earnest as the hour
That calls the noisy world to grateful sleep,
Our silent thought reveres the nameless power
That high seclusion round thy life doth keep:
So, feigned the poets, did Diana love
To smile upon her darlings while they slept;
Serene, untouched, and walking far above
The narrow ways wherein the many crept,
Along her lovely path of luminous air
She glided, of her brightness unaware.

Yet if they said she heeded not the hymn
Of shepherds gazing heavenward from the moor;
Or homeward sailors, when the waters dim

Flashed with long splendors, widening toward the
      shore ;
Nor wondering eyes of children cared to see ;
Or glowing face of happy lover, upturned,
As late he wended from the trysting-tree,
Lit by the kindly lamp in heaven that burned ;
And heard unmoved the prayer of wakeful pain,
Or consecrated maiden's holy vow, —
Believe them not : they sing the song in vain ;
For so it never was, and is not now.
Her heart was gentle as her face was fair,
With grace and love and pity dwelling there.

EMERSON

LONELY these meadows green,
Silent these warbling woodlands must appear
To us, by whom our Poet-sage was seen
Wandering among their beauties, year by year, —
Listening with delicate ear
To each fine note that fell from tree or sky,
Or rose from earth on high, —
Glancing his falcon eye,
In kindly radiance, as of some young star,
At all the shows of Nature near and far,

Or on the tame procession plodding by
Of daily toil and care, — and all Life's pagean-
       try ;
Then darting forth warm beams of wit and love,
Wide as the sun's great orbit, and as high above
These paths wherein our lowly tasks we ply.

His was the task and his the lordly gift
Our eyes, our hearts, bent earthward, to uplift ;
He found us chained in Plato's fabled cave,
Our faces long averted from the blaze
Of Heaven's broad light, and idly turned to gaze
On shadows, flitting ceaseless as the wave
That dashes ever idly on some isle enchanted ;
By shadows haunted
We sat, — amused in youth, in manhood daunted,
In vacant age forlorn, — then slipped within the
       grave,
The same dull chain still clasped around our
       shroud.
These captives, bound and bowed,
He from their dungeon like that angel led,
Who softly to imprisoned Peter said,
" Arise up quickly ! gird thyself and flee ! "
We wist not whose the thrilling voice, we knew
       our souls were free.

Ah! blest those years of youthful hope,
When every breeze was zephyr, every morning
    May!
Then, as we bravely climbed the slope
Of life's steep mount, we gained a wider scope
At every stair, — and could with joy survey
The track beneath us, and the upward way;
Both lay in light, — round both the breath of
    love
Fragrant and warm from Heaven's own tropic
    blew;
Beside us what glad comrades smiled and strove!
Beyond us what dim visions rose to view!
With thee, dear Master, through that morning
    land
We journeyed happy; thine the guiding hand,
Thine the far-looking eye, the dauntless smile;
Thy lofty song of hope did the long march be-
    guile.

Now scattered wide and lost to loving sight
The gallant train
That heard thy strain!
' T is May no longer, — shadows of the night
Beset the downward path, thy light withdrawn, —
And with thee vanished that perpetual dawn

Of which thou wert the harbinger and seer.
Yet courage! comrades, — though no more we
    hear
Each other's voices, lost within this cloud
That Time and Chance about our way have cast, —
Still his brave music haunts the hearkening ear,
As 'mid bold cliffs and dewy passes of the Past
Be that our countersign! for chanting loud,
His magic song, though far apart we go,
Best shall we thus discern both friend and foe.

John Albee

ARS POETICA ET HUMANA

Dost thou, belovèd, see
That even poesy
Hath rights like thine and mine?
   Dost thou its harmonies
   Observe, and how there lies
Along the builded line
   The touch, the frequent ties
The muses love to twine?

See, at the very end
The loving words must blend
In 'cording rhymes, and kiss,
Their meaning not to miss,
Ere they onward flow
Some other mood to show.
   So do our hearts rehearse,
      In earnest or in play,
   The self-same pulse-like verse,
      And lips seal what lips say.

JOHN ALBEE

MUSIC AND MEMORY

ENCHANTRESS, touch no more that strain !
I know not what it may contain,
But in my breast such mood it wakes
My very spirit almost breaks.
Thoughts come from out some hidden realm
Whose dim memorials overwhelm,
Still bring not back the things I lost, —
Still bringing all the pain they cost.

REMEMBERED LOVE

As two birds journeying from different lands
   Rest in the green-leafed tree, then hold their
      way,
Each for some other home where fate commands,
   So stayed, so passed two souls one blissful day.

Now hope and fear are dead — nor all, nor quite,
   For oft in dreams returns to me more sweet,
Like distant music in a summer night,
   The love that bound me captive at her feet.

REMEMBERED LOVE

All passions, all desires return no more ;
   The beauty and the worth in her I loved
Remade the world, and opened wide the door
   To realms of thought with calmer beauty moved.

Joel Benton

THE POET

THE poet's words are winged with fire,
Forever young is his desire, —
Touched by some charm the gods impart,
Time writes no wrinkles on his heart.

The messenger and priest of truth,
His thought breathes of immortal youth;
Though summer hours are far away,
Midsummer haunts him day by day.

The harsh fates do not chill his soul, —
For him all streams of splendor roll;
Sweet hints come to him from the sky, —
Birds teach him wisdom as they fly.

He gathers good in all he meets,
The fields pour out for him their sweets;
Life is excess; one sunset's glow
Gives him a bliss no others know.

Beauty to him is Paradise —
He never tires of lustrous eyes;
Quaffing his joy, the world apart,
Love lives a summer in his heart.

His lands are never bought or sold —
His wealth is more to him than gold;
On the green hills, when life is done,
He sleeps like fair Endymion.

THE WHIPPOORWILL

In the summer nights, when the world's tumult
    stills,
I hear at the wood's edge the whippoorwill's
Quaint, plaintive-phrased, monotonous refrain,
Flooding with pathos vale and dell and plain.

Silent until the setting of the sun,
He sings when the day's choristry is done,
With palpitant burst of rhythm and iterant rhyme
Rich with the redolent grace of summer-time.

Shy recluse of the woods and shaded streams,
Recaller of our life's youth-haloed dreams,

Brown portent that securely baffles sight,
Sacred to Wonder and Mysterious Night.

How alien to the din of city streets
Are all thy notes and twilight-kissed retreats!
That song of rapture, weird yet exquisite,
Who shall explain — who try to fathom it?

It tells of bosky haunts and fields of peace,
Of dew-wet meadows, and the day's surcease;
Of happy homes beyond that fast-closed door
Entombing childhood which returns no more.

WELTSCHMERZ

The child-eyed wonder with which life began,
  The prattling voice of joy, the heart of glee,
Have followed not the footsteps of the man;
  A world more sorrowful it is that he
Must battle with, and fearlessly explore:
  Far fades the gleam of Life's once purpled sea
When Youth was ours — the Youth that comes
      no more.

Those happy shores retreat which once we knew;
  The well-loved voices, hushed and still are they;

WELTSCHMERZ

Lost halcyon years, with skies of deepest blue,
　　Dear hearts that vanished some sad yesterday
Leave our life's journey dark.　Alas, how true
　　This deep World-Sorrow shadows all our way!

Yet somewhere, to some unknown, far-off strand,
　　Whose silver coast beyond the horizon's rim
　　　　Gleams with sweet promise, they　perchance
　　　　　　have passed,
　　Where all is plain which now seems dark and
　　　　dim;
And when we reach it we shall understand
　　　　The mystery — the puzzle real at last —
And find beyond these shadows and shed tears
The perfect joy of Heaven's untarnished years.

Augusta Cooper Bristol

A SUMMER MORNING HOUR WITH NATURE

The Night has gathered up her moonlit fringes,
  And curtains gray,
And orient gates, that move on silver hinges,
  Let in the day.

The morning sun his golden eye-lash raises
  O'er eastern hills;
The happy summer bird, with matin praises
  The thicket fills.

And Nature's dress, with softly tinted roses,
  And lilies wrought,
Through all its varied unity discloses
  God's perfect thought.

Great Nature! hand in hand with her I travel
  Adown the mead,

And half her precious mysteries unravel,
    Her scripture read.

And while the soft wind lifts her tinted pages,
    And turns them o'er,
My heart goes back to one in bygone ages
    Who loved her lore,

And symbols used of harvest field, and fountain,
    And breezy air;
Who sought the sacred silence of the mountain,
    For secret prayer.

Oh drop, my soul, the burden that oppresses,
    And cares that rule,
That I may prove the whispering wildernesses
    Heaven's vestibule!

For I can hear, despite material warden
    And earthly locks,
A still small voice; and know that through His
      garden
    The Father walks.

The fragrant lips of dewy flowers that glisten
    Along the sward,

Are whispering to my spirit as I listen,
  "It is the Lord."

And forest monarchs tell by reverent gesture
  And solemn sigh,
That the veiled splendor of His awful vesture
  Is passing by.

The billows witness Him. No more they darkle,
  But leap to lave
The silent marching feet, that leave a sparkle
  Along the wave.

And sweet aromas, fresher and intenser,
  The gales refine ;
The odor floating from the lily's censer
  Is breath divine.

Thus Nature, Heaven's voice, yields precious wit-
    ness,
  And large reply,
To him who comes to her with inward fitness
  Of harmony.

SOMEWHERE

SOMEWHERE await the treasures we have strewn,
  Which idle hands and feet have rudely shat-
      tered ;
And tenderest love shall gather as its own
    The pearls thus scattered.

Somewhere the tears of broken-hearted trust,
  Of patient sacrifice and self-submission,
Shall form the rainbow promise of a just
    And full fruition.

Somewhere the narrow stepping-stones we tread —
  The steep and terrible ascent of Duty —
Shall change to velvet terraces, o'erspread
    With emerald beauty.

Somewhere the doubtful seed that we have sown
  Shall well disprove a cold, uncertain rootage,
And vindicate the hope we now disown
    By fairest fruitage.

Somewhere our human effort of to-day,
   The faltering outcome of a pure intention,
Eternity shall hold as brave assay
     And true ascension.

O Universal Soul!   The finite range
   Of earth and time may dwarf our high en-
     deavor,
Yet Life is victory, through the evolving change
   Of thy Forever.

THE OLD SONG AND THE NEW

THE OLD

CLOSE are the shadows and dim is the day;
   God is away from the world!
Twilight encloseth the finite for aye;
   God is away from the world!
Outward Humanity leaneth in vain,
Straining her vision a witness to gain
Of the background being — the infinite plain; —
   God is away from the world!

He hath no part in the voices of earth;
   God is away from the world!

Man hath appraised them, and noted their worth;
   God is away from the world!
Gather the sounds of the sea and the air,
Harmonies subtle, and symphonies rare, —
Still not a whisper from Deity there;
   God is away from the world!

Vainly we seek with the eye and the ear;
   God is away from the world!
His vesture and footprints no longer appear;
   God is away from the world!
He cometh no more with a daily accost
To the finite; the garden is cold with the frost,
And the echoes of Eden forever are lost:
   God is away from the world.

Heaven hath no actual commerce with man;
   God is away from the world!
He hath perfected His purpose and plan;
   God is away from the world!
Creation is finished; He sitteth apart,
In a glory too dread for the scene of His art;
Too piercingly pure for Humanity's heart;
   God is away from the world!

Truth is not ours, in its absolute ray; —
   God is away from the world!

Only poor gleams of the actual day;
   God is away from the world!
We reach not the substance; we touch but the
     screen;
Our hope is the victim that 's lifted between
The real and the seeming, the Christ-Nazarene;
   God is away from the world!

THE NEW

Heirs of the Morning, we walk in the light;
   God is forever with man!
A day that hath never a noon or a night;
   God is forever with man!
A day without limit, whose glories unfold
The statutes that time and eternity hold;
An endless becoming its measure and mould;
   God is forever with man!

He sitteth a guest in Humanity's soul;
   God is forever with man!
Life leadeth on to an infinite goal;
   God is forever with man!
Inward, not outward, is Deity's shrine,
The Presence Eternal — the Spirit Divine,
And being becomes immortality's sign;
   God is forever with man!

THE OLD SONG AND THE NEW

Truth is not veiled to mortality's eye;
  God is forever with man!
We have a witness on which to rely;
  God is forever with man!
The word is eternal, and cometh to all;
And the inward rebuke, and the heart's ceaseless call,
Are tones from the lips of the Father that fall;
  God is forever with man!

Of all that is real the human hath part;
  God is forever with man!
Our roots are the veins of the Infinite Heart;
  God is forever with man!
The Christ liveth ever in creature disguise;
The Logos by which every soul shall arise
The gospel and glory of self-sacrifice;
  God is forever with man!

Sing, little bluebird, the message ye bring;
  God is forever with man!
Cleave the soft air with a rapturous wing;
  God is forever with man!
Warble the story to forest and rill,
Sweep up the valley and bear to the hill
The sacred refrain of your passionate trill;
  God is forever with man!

Open bright roses, and blossom the thought;
  God is forever with man!
Precious the meaning your beauty hath wrought;
  God is forever with man!
Spread out the sweet revelation of bloom,
Lift and release from an odorous tomb,
The secret embalmed in a honeyed perfume;
  God is forever with man!

Dance, happy billow, and say to the shore,
  God is forever with man!
Echo, sea-caverns, the truth evermore,
  God is forever with man!
Bear on, Creation, the symbol and sign,
That being unfolds in an aura divine,
The soul moveth on in an infinite line;
  God is forever with man!

ART–SERVICE

I WANDERED with an earnest heart
  Among the quarried depths of Thought,
And kindled by the poet's art,
    I deftly wrought.

I wrought for Beauty; and the world
　　Grew very green and smooth for me,
And blossom-banners hung unfurled
　　　On every tree.

Upon my heated forehead lay
　　The cooling laurel, and my feet
Crushed honeyed fragrance out, the way
　　　Had grown so sweet.

And praise was servant of the ear,
　　And love dropped kisses on the cheek,
And smiled a passion-thought too dear
　　　For tongue to speak.

But one day the ideal Good
　　Baptized me with immortal youth;
And in sublimity of mood
　　　I wrought for Truth.

Oh then, instead of laurel crown
　　The world entwined a thorny band,
And on my forehead pressed it down
　　　With heavy hand.

And looks that used to warm me, froze;
　　I lost the cheer, the odor sweet,

The path of velvet; glaciers rose
    Before my feet.

Yet Truth the more divinely shone,
    As onward still I sought to press,
And gloriously proved her own
    Almightiness.

For girded in her cuirass strong,
    And lifted by her matchless arm,
Above the frozen peak of Wrong,
    In warmth and calm,

I sit, and white thoughts, lily pure,
    Like angels, close my heart around,
And fold me gently in, secure
    From cold or wound.

O kindred poet-soul, whose lays
    Of sweet word-music set in line
Are fashioned for the world's poor praise
    And Beauty's shrine, —

The martyr's spirit-wing is strong!
    Choose thou a pinion that can rise
With Truth's full freight of clarion-song
    And sweep the skies!

Then shall the thoughts that in thee burn,
  Flame-reaching, touch the thought divine;
And man may scoff, a world may spurn,
  But Heaven is thine.

Anna Callender Brackett

BEETHOVEN

Lo, the strong eagle, through the storm and night,
    Up-winging to the light,
Sea-bound, as fitful rose along the shore
    The low, deep roar
Of rising wind, and many-voiced, the sea
    Moaned answer fitfully.

Adown from cloud to cloud the drooping sun
    Drew near the horizon dun;
A ray of sunshine, then a shade again,
    Till over all the unquiet main
Came down the doubtful shadow round his flight,
    And deepened into night.

Dimly white-crested, lashing waves rose high
    Against the stormy sky;
Full on his breast the angry blasts drove keen
    With scarce a breath between,
And hurrying clouds but let a star shine through,
    To vanish quickly too.

Till down upon the raging sea, the rain,
  Like pain to quiet pain,
Came, driven by the scourging blasts of wind,
  Still following close behind,
And mocking waves plucked at his onward flight
  Through tempest and through night.

Yet still the beat of his strong pinions gave,
  Through dashing wind and wave,
Their measure to the slow-paced hours, and still
  Do find all powers of ill ;
Alone, the patient pinions cleft the air,
  Nor drooped once in despair.

So hour by hour the long night wore away,
  And blossomed into day.
At last ! at last !   The morning breaks at last !
  The night and storm are past ;
On broad-browed headlands sleeps the sunlight free,
  And there is no more sea !

At last upon the bravely throbbing breast,
  The cleaving wings may rest.
O tireless pinions ! Ye have won the light
  Through tempest and through night.
O'er all the waves of time for us your echoes beat
  In music strong and sweet.

FOUR WHITE LILIES

'T WAS a vision, a dream of the night,
  When deep sleep falleth on man ;
Out of the shadowless darkness it glided
  Into shadowless darkness again.

Afloat upon silentest waters
  On the smooth, slow waves I lay,
And through them I saw, but dimly,
  The round white lilies sway.

Then I reached down my careful fingers,
  And drew them, one by one,
Out of the smoky water
  Up into the shine of the sun.

White-bosomed and golden-hearted,
  And sweet — for I tried, to see, —
I drew them by slippery stemlets,
  One by one, up to me.

Then I turned on my side, and broke them,
  Stem by stem, with my teeth,

But the broad green leaves I left floating
In the water underneath.

I blew open the pink-white petals
To the yellow-dusted core,
And I counted them as I held them,
One, and two, and three, and four.

Then they drooped their heads as weary
Till the cool petals touched my hand —
Did I drop them into the water?
Did I ever float to land? —

Who knows?   Out of shadowless darkness
To shadowless darkness they grew,
But they haunt me, my four white lilies
Till I gather them anew.

DENIAL

THE two best gifts in all the perfect world
Lie in two close-shut hands;
The hands rest even on the outstretched knees
Like those stone forms the 'wildered traveller sees
In dreamy Eastern lands.

I reach to grasp : but lo ! that hand withdraws, —
    The other forward glides ;
The silent gesture says : " This is for thee,
Take now and wait not ever, listlessly,
    For changing times and tides."

I take — Thou canst not say I took it not !
    The record readeth fair.
I take and use, and come again to crave,
With weary hands and feet, but spirit brave —
    The same thing lieth there.

So many times ! ah me ! so many times !
    The same hand gives the gift ;
And must I, till the evening shadows grow,
Still kneel before an everlasting No,
    To see the other lift ?

I ask for bread ; Thou givest me a stone ;
    Oh, give the other now !
Thou knowest, Thou, the spirit's bitter need,
The day grows sultry as I come to plead
    With dust on hand and brow.

Ah fool ! Is he not greater than thy heart ?
    His eyes are kindest still.

COMPREHENSION

And seeing all, He surely knoweth best;
Oh, if no other, know the perfect rest
    Of yielding to His will.

Perchance — He knows — canst thou not trust
        His love?
    For no expectant eyes
Of something other, full of wild desire
Can watch the burning of the altar fire
    Of daily sacrifice.

COMPREHENSION

    Foot surer than his, crossing o'er
    The rapid river shore to shore
    While down the stream the ice-floes roar, —

    Hold closer than the bird's that sings
    Unmindful how the storm-wind swings
    The slender twig to which he clings, —

    Touch finer far than that so fine
    Upon the spider's silvery line
    He crosses sure through sun and shine, —
                283

O surer, closer, finer yet,
Must be the thought that strives to get
And hold the Truth inviolate.

For narrow as the bridge did rise
Before the prophet's wondering eyes,
Runs still the path to Paradise.

On either side we seize despair ;
We prison fast the sunlit air,
And lo ! ' tis darkness that is there !

And so we miss, and grasp, and lose,
While Thought its shadow still pursues,
Nor knows its work is not to choose ;

For only where the one is twain,
And where the two are one again,
Will Truth no more be sought in vain.

Francis Ellingwood Abbot

GODWARD

Thou Soul that overlightest mine!
That with Thy solar blaze divine
Quenchest the firefly's timid shine!

Shall Thy vast lustre be my night?
A spark burns here, — and light is light;
I am of Thee, O Infinite!

For Thou and I are next of kin;
The pulses that are strong within,
From the deep Infinite heart begin.

Thou art my All, — but what am I?
A flickering hope, a passionate sigh
Exhaled upon the kindred sky.

Ah, not in vain the cry shall be!
In these poor shoots of flame I see
A burning effluence from Thee;

And tending towards Thee ever higher,
Their hearts shall evermore aspire
To mix with Thee, Empyreal Fire!

MATINS

SLOWLY the sun climbs up the amber east,
   And from her mountain-altars broad
Earth rolls aloft pale wreaths of curling mist, —
      Incense to God.

Hark to the anthem of the low-voiced sea!
   Along the distant-dying strand
Whisper the billowy choir their symphony,
      Vast, deep, and grand.

Through his wild forest-harp of piny strings
   Soft breathes the wind melodious strains,
And piping birds pour forth their jargonings
      In leafy fanes.

Earth, sea and air their sweetest notes employ
   To hymn thy praise, O Holy One!
And chant perpetual songs of grateful joy
      Before thy throne.

But my mute awe can find no voice or tongue —
  Silent the waves of worship roll ;
Yet poor, discordant, weak, Thou hear'st a song
    Deep in my soul.

A BIRTH–DAY PRAYER

  ART Thou the Life ?
To Thee, then, do I owe each beat and breath,
And wait Thy ordering of the hour of death,
    In peace or strife.

  Art Thou the Light ?
To Thee, then, in the sunshine or the cloud,
Or in my chamber lone or in the crowd,
    I lift my sight.

  Art Thou the Truth ?
To Thee, then, loved and craved and sought of
        yore,
I consecrate my manhood o'er and o'er,
    As once my youth.

  Art Thou the Strong ?
To Thee, then, though the air is thick with night,
I trust the seeming unprotected Right,
    And leave the Wrong.

Art Thou the Wise?
To Thee, then, do I bring each useless care,
And bid my soul unsay her idle prayer,
    And hush her cries.

Art Thou the Good?
To Thee, then, with a thirsting heart I turn,
And stand, and at Thy fountain hold my urn,
    As aye I stood.

Forgive the call!
I cannot shut Thee from my sense or soul,
I cannot lose me in thy boundless whole, —
    For Thou art All!

John White Chadwick

NIRVANA

ALONG the scholar's glowing page
  I read the Orient thinker's dream
  Of things that are not what they seem,
Of mystic chant and Soma's rage.

The sunlight flooding all the room
  To me again was Indra's smile,
  And on the hearth the blazing pile
For Agni's sake did fret and fume.

Yet most I read of who aspire
  To win Nirvana's deep repose, —
  Of that long way the spirit goes
To reach the absence of desire.

But through the music of my book
  Another music smote my ear, —
  A tinkle silver-sweet and clear, —
The babble of the mountain-brook.

"Oh! leave," it said, "your ancient seers;
  Come out into the woods with me;
  Behold an older mystery
Than Buddhist's hope or Brahman's fears!"

The voice so sweet I could but hear.
  I sallied forth with staff in hand,
  Where, mile on mile, the mountain land
Was radiant with the dying year.

I heard the startled partridge whirr,
  And crinkling through the tender grass
  I saw the stripèd adder pass,
Where dropped the chestnut's prickly burr.

I saw the miracle of life
  From death upspringing evermore;
  The fallen tree a forest bore
Of tiny forms with beauty rife.

I gathered mosses rare and sweet,
  The acorn in its carven cup;
  'Mid heaps of leaves, wind-gathered up,
I trod with half-remorseful feet.

The maple's blush I made my own,
  The sumac's crimson splendor bold,

The poplar's hue of paly gold,
The faded chestnut, crisp and brown.

I climbed the mountain's shaggy crest,
  Where masses huge of molten rock,
  After long years of pain and shock,
Fern-covered, from their wanderings rest.

Far, far below the valley spread
  Its rich, roof-dotted, wide expanse;
  And further still the sunlight's dance
The amorous river gayly led.

But still, with all I heard or saw
  There mingled thoughts of that old time,
  And that enchanted Eastern clime
Where Buddha gave his mystic law, —

Till, wearied with the lengthy way,
  I found a spot where all was still,
  Just as the sun behind the hill
Was making bright the parting day.

On either side the mountains stood,
  Masses of color rich and warm;
  And over them, in giant form,
The rosy moon serenely glowed.

My heart was full as it could hold ;
  The Buddha's paradise was mine ;
  My mountain-nook its inmost shrine,
The fretted sky its roof of gold.

Nirvana's peace my soul had found, —
  Absence complete of all desire, —
  While the great moon was mounting higher,
And deeper quiet breathed around.

A SONG OF TRUST

O Love Divine, of all that is
  The sweetest still and best,
Fain would I come and rest to-night
  Upon thy sheltering breast.

As tired of sin as any child
  Was ever tired of play,
When evening's hush has folded in
  The noises of the day ;

When just for very weariness
  The little one will creep
Into the arms that have no joy
  Like holding him in sleep ;

And looking upward to Thy face,
   So gentle, sweet, and strong
In all its looks for those who love,
   So pitiful of wrong.

I pray Thee turn me not away,
   For, sinful though I be,
Thou knowest every thing I need
   And all my need of Thee.

And yet the spirit in my heart
   Says, Wherefore should I pray
That Thou shouldst seek me with Thy love,
   Since Thou dost seek alway?

And dost not even wait until
   I urge my steps to Thee;
But in the darkness of my life
   Art coming still to me.

I pray not, then, because I would;
   I pray because I must;
There is no meaning in my prayer
   But thankfulness and trust.

I would not have Thee otherwise
   Than what Thou ever art;

Be still Thyself, and then I know
    We cannot live apart.

But still Thy love will beckon me,
    And still Thy strength will come,
In many ways to bear me up
    And bring me to my home.

And Thou wilt hear the thought I mean,
    And not the words I say;
Wilt hear the thanks among the words
    That only seem to pray;

As if Thou wert not always good,
    As if Thy loving care
Could even miss me in the midst
    Of this Thy temple fair.

If ever I have doubted Thee,
    How can I any more,
So quick to-night my tossing bark
    Has reached the happy shore;

And, even while it sighed, my heart
    Has sung itself to rest,
O Love Divine, forever near,
    Upon Thy sheltering breast!

AULD LANG SYNE

It singeth low in every heart,
  We hear it each and all, —
A song of those who answer not,
  However we may call;
They throng the silence of the breast,
  We see them as of yore, —
The kind, the brave, the true, the sweet,
  Who walk with us no more.

'T is hard to take the burden up,
  When these have laid it down;
They brightened all the joy of life,
  They softened every frown;
But oh, 't is good to think of them,
  When we are troubled sore!
Thanks be to God that such have been,
  Although they are no more!

More home-like seems the vast unknown,
  Since they have entered there;
To follow them were not so hard,
  Wherever they may fare;

295

They cannot be where God is not,
   On any sea or shore;
Whate'er betides, Thy love abides,
   Our God, for evermore.

William Channing Gannett

"WHO WERT AND ART AND EVER-MORE SHALT BE"

BRING, O Morn, thy music!   Bring, O Night, thy
    huskes!
  Oceans, laugh the rapture to the storm-winds
    coursing free!
Suns and stars are singing, Thou art Creator,
  Who wert, and art, and evermore shalt be!

Life and Death, thy creatures, praise thee, Mighty
    Giver!
  Praise and prayer are rising in thy beast and
    bird and tree:
Lo! they praise and vanish, vanish at thy bid-
    ding, —
  Who wert, and art, and evermore shalt be!

Light us! lead us! love us! cry thy groping na-
    tions,
  Pleading in the thousand tongues but naming
    only thee,

297

Weaving blindly out thy holy, happy purpose, —
  Who wert, and art, and evermore shalt be!

Life nor Death can part us, O thou Love Eter-
    nal,
  Shepherd of the wandering star and souls that
      wayward flee!
Homeward draws the spirit to thy Spirit yearn-
    ing, —
  Who wert, and art, and evermore shalt be!

THE HIGHWAY

"Whatever road I take joins the highway that leads to thee."

WHEN the night is still and far,
  Watcher from the shadowed deeps!
When the morning breaks its bar,
  Life that shines and wakes and leaps!
When old Bible-verses glow,
  Starring all the deep of thought,
Till it fills with quiet dawn
    From the peace our years have brought, —
      Sun within both skies, we see
      How all lights lead back to thee!

'Cross the field of daily work
  Run the footpaths, leading — where?
Run they east or run they west,
  One way all the workers fare.
Every awful thing of earth, —
  Sin and pain and battle-noise;
Every dear thing, — baby's birth,
  Faces, flowers, or lovers' joys, —
    Is a wicket-gate, where we
    Join the great highway to thee!

Restless, restless, speed we on, —
  Whither in the vast unknown?
Not to you and not to me
  Are the sealèd orders shown:
But the Hand that built the road,
  And the Light that leads the feet,
And this inward restlessness,
  Are such invitation sweet,
    That where I no longer see,
    Highway still must lead to thee!

THE WORD OF GOD

It sounds along the ages,
  Soul answering to soul;

It kindles on the pages
  Of every Bible scroll;
The psalmists heard and sang it,
  From martyr-lips it broke,
And prophet-tongues outrang it
  Till sleeping nations woke.

From Sinai's cliffs it echoed,
  It breathed from Buddha's tree,
It charmed in Athens' market,
  It gladdened Galilee;
The hammer-stroke of Luther,
  The Pilgrims' seaside prayer,
The oracles of Concord,
  One holy Word declare.

It dates each new ideal, —
  Itself it knows not time:
Man's laws but catch the music
  Of its eternal chime.
It calls — and lo, new Justice!
  It speaks — and lo, new Truth!
In ever nobler stature
  And unexhausted youth.

It everywhere arriveth;
   Recks not of small and great;
It shapes the unborn atom,
   It tells the sun its fate.
The wingbeat of archangel
   Its boundary nevei nears:
Forever on it soundeth
   The music of the spheres!

LISTENING FOR GOD

I HEAR it often in the dark,
   I hear it in the light, —
Where is the voice that calls to me
   With such a quiet might?
It seems but echo to my thought,
   And yet beyond the stars;
It seems a heart-beat in a hush,
   And yet the planet jars!

O, may it be that far within
   My inmost soul there lies
A spirit-sky, that opens with
   Those voices of surprise?

And can it be, by night and day,
  That firmament serene
Is just the heaven where God himself,
  The Father, dwells, unseen?

O God, within, so close to me
  That every thought is plain,
Be judge, be friend, be Father still,
  And in thy heaven reign!
Thy heaven is mine, — my very soul!
  Thy words are sweet and strong,
They fill my inward silences
  With music and with song.

They send me challenges to right
  And loud rebuke my ill;
They ring my bells of victory,
  They breathe my " Peace, be still!"
They ever seem to say: My child,
  Why seek me so all day?
Now journey inward to thyself,
  And listen by the way!

Frederick Lucian Hosmer

THE THOUGHT OF GOD

ONE thought I have, my ample creed,
    So deep it is and broad,
And equal to my every need, —
    It is the thought of God.

Each morn unfolds some fresh surprise,
    I feast at life's full board;
And rising in my inner skies
    Shines forth the thought of God.

At night my gladness is my prayer;
    I drop my daily load,
And every care is pillowed there
    Upon the thought of God.

I ask not far before to see,
    But take in trust my road;
Life, death, and immortality
    Are in my thought of God.

To this their secret strength they owed
   The martyr's path who trod ;
The fountains of their patience flowed
   From out their thought of God.

Be still the light upon my way,
   My pilgrim staff and rod,
My rest by night, my strength by day,
   O blessèd thought of God!

THE MYSTERY OF GOD

O Thou, in all thy might so far,
   In all thy love so near,
Beyond the range of sun and star,
   And yet beside us here, —

What heart can comprehend Thy name,
   Or searching, find Thee out,
Who art within a quickening Flame,
   A Presence round about?

Yet though I know Thee but in part,
   I ask not, Lord, for more :
Enough for me to know Thou art,
   To love Thee and adore.

O sweeter than aught else besides,
 The tender mystery
That like a veil of shadow hides
 The Light I may not see!

And dearer than all things I know
 Is childlike faith to me,
That makes the darkest way I go
 An open path to Thee.

NOTES

NOTES

RALPH WALDO EMERSON. Born in Boston, May 25, 1803; died in Concord, Mass., April 27, 1885. He was the real leader of the transcendental movement, and in his books will be found its best interpretation. "Each and All," and "The Rhodora," were first printed in "The Western Messenger," edited by James Freeman Clarke, and published in Louisville, Ky., 1839. With "The Humble-Bee," and "Good-bye, proud world," published in the same journal, they were the earliest of his poems to appear in print. "The Problem" was printed in the first number of "The Dial;" and in the same journal appeared "Woodnotes," the concluding part of which is given here as "The Eternal Pan." "Fate" was also printed in "The Dial," and is included, slightly changed, in his poems, under the title "Destiny."

JAMES RUSSELL LOWELL. Born in Cambridge, February 22, 1819; died there August 12, 1891. In his early life he was largely influenced by transcendentalism, as the first volume of his biography by Horace E. Scudder amply indicates. The first three sonnets selected were printed in "The Dial," from which they are taken. The fourth sonnet, and "Winter," appeared in "The Present," edited in New York by Rev. William Henry

NOTES

Channing, 1843–44. "Love Reflected in Nature" and "The Street" were printed in "The Pioneer," edited by Lowell in Boston, 1843. "Bibliolatres" is from the poem of that name, and "Divine Teachers" is the introductory part of "Rhœcus."

AMOS BRONSON ALCOTT. Born in Wolcott, Conn., November 29, 1799; died in Boston, March 4, 1888. He was a teacher in Cheshire, Boston, and Philadelphia; returned to Boston, and became widely known by his "Temple School" and its methods. Then resided in Concord as the neighbor of Emerson, held conversations, and became famous for his philosophical teachings. He was a contributor to "The Dial," "The Western Messenger," "The Radical," and other periodicals. His "Orphic Sayings," and other philosophical writings, were much discussed, and frequently satirized. He was the founder of the Concord School of Philosophy, and his last years were largely devoted to its interests and to the lectures he gave before it. "Matter" was first published in "Table-Talk," 1877; the other poems in "Tablets," 1868; and the sonnets in "Sonnets and Canzonets," 1882.

HENRY DAVID THOREAU. Born in Concord, Mass., July 12, 1817; died there, May 6, 1862. Graduated at Harvard, 1837; taught school, and lectured. He lived in Emerson's family, and was largely influenced by him. Was a contributor to "The Dial," and helped Emerson edit the last two volumes. He wrote for other periodicals, and was for a time tutor in the family of

William Emerson on Staten Island. From 1843 to
1845 he lived alone in a hut on the shore of Walden
Pond, in Concord. In 1849 he published " A Week on
the Concord and Merrimac Rivers ; " and, in 1854,
" Walden, or Life in the Woods." His other books
appeared after his death, edited by his friends. " Stan-
zas," " My Prayer," " Rumors from an Æolian Harp,"
and " Inward Morning " were first printed in " The
Dial ; " " Conscience," " Lines," and " My Life " were
included in " A Week," and " Inspiration " in the volume
of " Miscellanies." His poems have been edited by
Henry S. Salt and Frank B. Sanborn under the title of
" Poems of Nature."

MARGARET FULLER. Born in Cambridge, May 23,
1810 ; died off Fire Island beach, July 16, 1850. She
was a teacher in Providence, Boston, and elsewhere ;
held conversations in Boston that attracted attention to
her genius ; and was the editor of " The Dial " for the
first two years of its existence. Then she was con-
nected with the New York " Tribune," 1844–47. In
1847 she went to Europe, and the next year married
the Marquis of Ossoli. The vessel on which she sailed
for home was lost off the coast of Long Island. " Life
a Temple " was published at the end of " Life With-
out and Life Within," 1859. " Encouragement " was
printed in the extracts from letters and journals that
were appended to the edition of " Woman in the Nine-
teenth Century," 1855. " Sub Rosa, Crux " was first
printed in " Summer on the Lakes," and is, according

to Colonel T. W. Higginson, "her most thoughtful and artistic poem; almost the only one of hers to which the last epithet could be applied, if, indeed, it be applicable here. It is on a theme which suited her love of mystic colors and symbols — the tradition of the Rosicrucians. The modern theory is, however, that this word did not come from the cross and the rose, as she assumes, but from the cross and the dew (*ros*); this last substance being then considered as the most powerful solvent of gold, and so used in the effort to discover the philosopher's stone." The "Dryad Song" evidently expresses the faith that made Margaret Fuller say, "I *know* that I am immortal."

CHRISTOPHER PEARSE CRANCH. Born in Alexandria, Va., March 8, 1813; died in Cambridge, January 20, 1892. He studied at Columbian College and Harvard Divinity School, preached in Unitarian churches for a short time without settlement, then became a painter, and lived in Paris, New York, and Cambridge. He wrote largely for periodicals, and published "Poems," 1844; translation of the "Æneid," 1872; "Satan, a Libretto," 1874; "The Bird and the Bell, and other Poems," 1875; "Ariel and Caliban, with other Poems," 1887. His "Gnosis," "Correspondences," and "The Ocean" first appeared in "The Dial." In that periodical the title of "Gnosis" was "Stanzas."

WILLIAM ELLERY CHANNING. Nephew of Dr. Channing, after whom he was named, born in Boston, June 10, 1818; died in Concord, Mass., December 23, 1901.

Most of his life was spent in Concord. He published "Poems," 1843; second series, 1847; "Conversations in Rome between an Artist, a Catholic, and a Critic," 1847; "Near Home: A Poem," 1858; "The Burial of John Brown," 1860; "The Wanderer: A Colloquial Poem," 1871; "The Poet Naturalist, with Memorial Verses," a biography of Thoreau, 1873; "Eliot, A Poem," 1885. Channing was one of the most frequent contributors of poetry to "The Dial," from which the first poem is selected. The last two are from "The Journal of Speculative Philosophy," and the others from his first two volumes of poems.

JAMES FREEMAN CLARKE. Born in Hanover, N. H., April 4, 1810; died in Boston, June 8, 1888. Graduated at Harvard and Divinity School, minister of Unitarian church in Louisville, Ky., then of Church of the Disciples in Boston, which he organized, from 1841 to his death. He published many theological, historical, and biographical works. He wrote but little poetry, but, with his daughter, published "Exotics," translations, mostly short poems from the German, in 1876. The poem selected was printed in "The Dial," and is used as a hymn in many collections. "You do not get a true estimate of Clarke," said Dr. F. H. Hedge, "unless you see him as a poet. He approached all subjects from the poetical side. This poetical habit of looking at everything gave him that fairness which you have observed. The rest of us have written as if we were philosophers. Clarke always wrote, no matter on how dull a subject, as a poet writes. And though he wrote few verses, it is because he is a poet that he has done what he has done."

FREDERIC HENRY HEDGE. Born in Cambridge, December 12, 1805; died there, August 21, 1890. Was settled over Unitarian churches in Arlington, Mass., Bangor, Me., Providence, R. I., and Brookline, Mass. In 1857 he became the professor of ecclesiastical history in the Harvard Divinity School, and in 1872 professor of the German language and literature in Harvard College. He published "Reason in Religion," 1865; "Ways of the Spirit," 1877, and several other works. He was one of the earliest Americans to study in Germany, and he accepted the transcendental philosophy with earnestness. The poem selected was printed in "The Dial," and has been frequently reprinted as "The Idealist." It was suggested to him while he was watching the stars during a sleepless night spent in a Bangor mail-coach, was composed under these circumstances, and written down upon reaching home.

JOHN SULLIVAN DWIGHT. Born in Boston, May 13, 1813; died there, September 5, 1893. Graduated at Harvard and Divinity School, preached in Unitarian churches a few years, was then a member of Brook Farm, and edited "Dwight's Journal of Music," in Boston, from 1852 to 1881. "To no one more than to him," wrote George William Curtis, "are we indebted for the intellectual taste which enjoys the best music. He was the earliest, and one of the best, of our critics of music." The first poem selected was printed in the first number of "The Dial," at the end of a paper on "The Religion of Beauty." The others first appeared in "The Harbinger," published at Brook Farm, of which George Ripley and Dwight were the editors.

ELIZA THAYER CLAPP. Born in Dorchester (Boston), November 13, 1811, and died there, February 26, 1888. She early came under the influence of Emerson, and contributed to "The Dial" several poems at his suggestion. She published two little books pervaded with the spirit of transcendentalism, in 1842 and 1845, and wrote occasionally for periodicals. She taught classes of girls and women in literature and philosophy. After her death, in 1888, was printed privately a little volume of her essays, letters, and poems. The first of the poems selected, printed in "The Dial," has been included in several collections of hymns and attributed to Emerson.

CHARLES TIMOTHY BROOKS. Born in Salem, June 20, 1813 ; died in Newport, June 14, 1883. Graduated at Harvard and Divinity School, and was settled over the Unitarian church in Newport from 1837 to 1873. He translated Goethe's "Faust," and many other poems, and published sermons and original poems.

ELLEN HOOPER. Born in Boston, February 17, 1812, and died there, November 3, 1848. She married Robert William Hooper, a Boston physician, her maiden name having been Sturgis. She was a frequent contributor to "The Dial," and an intimate friend of Margaret Fuller, Emerson, and other transcendentalists. No collection of her poems has been published, but they have been printed on sheets, inclosed in a portfolio, and given to her friends. Most of the poems selected appeared in "The Dial," and the others were printed in "The Disciples' Hymn Book," compiled by Rev. James Freeman Clarke for his church, and in Miss E. P. Peabody's "Æsthetic Papers." Emerson encouraged Mrs. Hooper to write, and had large expectations of her genius. Colonel T. W. Higginson described her as "a woman of genius," and Margaret Fuller wrote of her from Rome: "I have seen in Europe no woman more gifted by nature than she."

CAROLINE TAPPAN. Born in Boston in 1818 or 1819, and died there, October 20, 1888. She was a younger sister of Mrs. Hooper, and they were (and are) often spoken of as "the Sturgis sisters." She was one of Margaret Fuller's most intimate friends, and wrote largely for "The Dial," under her editorship; wrote two or three children's books; lived for many years at Lenox in the summer, and in the biographies of Hawthorne she is often mentioned. She was called "the American Bettine," probably because of a poem she printed in "The Dial." The poems selected were published in that journal. It is possible that the last poem was written by Mrs. Hooper.

CHARLES ANDERSON DANA. Born in Hinsdale, N. H., August 8, 1819; died in New York, October 17, 1897.

After studying for a time at Harvard, he was at Brook Farm nearly the whole period of its existence. Was assistant editor of the "New York Tribune." In 1868 he founded "The Sun" in New York, of which he was the editor until his death. He joined George Ripley in editing the "New American Cyclopedia," and he edited other works. The first three sonnets appeared in "The Dial;" "Ad Arma" in "The Present;" and "The Bankrupt" in "The Harbinger," published at Brook Farm. Other poems of Dana's were printed in "The Harbinger," but none of them are as good as those selected.

GEORGE WILLIAM CURTIS. Born in Providence, R. I., February 24, 1824; died on Staten Island, August 31, 1892. Studied at Brook Farm, travelled in Europe and the East, was connected with the "New York Tribune," an editor of "Putnam's Monthly," edited "Easy Chair" in "Harper's Monthly;" and was chief editorial writer in "Harper's Weekly." Author of "Nile Notes of a Howadji," 1851; "The Howadji in Syria," 1852; "Lotus-Eating," 1852; "Potiphar Papers," 1853; "Prue and I," 1856; "Trumps," 1862; and several volumes of his essays and orations have been published. He wrote only a few poems, and these have not been collected.

JONES VERY. Born in Salem, Mass., August 28, 1813; died there, May 8, 1880. Graduated at Harvard and Divinity School, but preached only occasionally, without being ordained. Tutor at Harvard for a few years, then retired to Salem, where most of his poems were written. Emerson edited his "Essays and Poems," in 1839. During his tutorship he was attacked with cerebral excitement approaching monomania, from which he never fully recovered. After his death his religious poems were edited by William P. Andrews, 1883; and Dr. J. F. Clarke published his complete poems and essays, 1886.

THEODORE PARKER. Born in Lexington, Mass., August 24, 1810; died in Florence, Italy, May 10, 1860. He was the great Unitarian preacher in Boston, the leader of the more radical wing of that denomination, an able lecturer, a prominent reformer. His sermons and lectures have been published in many volumes. He wrote but few poems, those selected being among the best. The last has been used in many hymn-books, with omission of last two lines.

SAMUEL GRAY WARD. Born in Boston, October 3, 1817, and is now living in Washington. He has been a banker in Boston and New York. In 1840 Ward published in Boston a volume of translations from Goethe, entitled "Essays on Art." He was an intimate friend of Emerson in his younger days, and Emerson's letters to him have been edited by Professor Charles Eliot Norton. Writing to Carlyle in 1843, Emerson described Ward as "my friend and the best man in the city, and, besides all his personal merits, a master of all the offices of hospitality." Emerson included three of Ward's poems in his "Parnassus." Ward wrote several prose articles for "The Dial," and the poems selected were printed there.

DAVID ATWOOD WASSON. Born in West Brookville, Me., May 14, 1823; died in West Medford, Mass., January 21, 1887. Studied at Bowdoin and Bangor Theological School, was then settled over the orthodox Congregational church in Groveland, Mass., became liberal, and an independent society was organized for him. In 1865–66 was minister of the church formed by Theodore Parker in Boston. For some years he had a position in the Boston Custom House, resided for a time in Germany, and then lived at West Medford, near Boston. He was a brilliant writer and lecturer. His essays, with memoir, were edited by O. B. Frothingham, 1888; and his poems by Mrs. Ednah D. Cheney, 1888. "All's Well" and "Seen and Unseen" were contributed to the early volumes of the "Atlantic Monthly," and the other poems selected appeared in "The Radical." The first line of "All's Well" is given as it was originally printed, and as it appears in the collected poems, edited by Mrs. Cheney. She says of this poem: "Written at sea, fifty days out, twelve hundred miles from the American shore. The long, tedious voyage, without the hoped-for benefit to his health, could not darken his hope or faith. Like the nightingale, his song gushed forth as the shadows gathered about him."

SYDNEY HENRY MORSE. Born in Rochester, N. Y., October 3, 1833. His youth was spent in New York, Connecticut, and Ohio. His education ended at thirteen, and he was taught the stone-cutter's trade. At about the age of twenty he went to Cincinnati, became acquainted with Moncure D. Conway, then minister of a Unitarian church in that city. In 1860 he went to Antioch College, which was closed on the opening of the Civil War. Then he preached for a few months at Fond du Lac, Wis., after which he went to Cambridge and carried on his studies in a desultory way, and preached when opportunity offered. He occupied Conway's pulpit for a year in Cincinnati, and was then settled over the Unitarian church in Haverhill, Mass. After the organization of the Unitarian National Conference on a basis that seemed to him too conservative, he began the publication of " The Radical " in Boston, with September, 1865; and it was continued through ten volumes, or for seven years. In the mean time he resigned his pulpit in Haverhill and abandoned the clerical profession. In 1872 he made a bust of Rip Van Winkle, and then one of Theodore Parker. These were followed by busts of Dr. Channing (now in the Arlington Street Church, Boston), Thomas Paine, Walt Whitman, Emerson (in Second Church, Boston), Lincoln, and others. He has written for the newspapers and lectured throughout the West. After spending some years in Chicago, he removed to Buffalo, where he now lives, occupied with a new bust of Emerson. All the poems selected were printed in " The Radical."

JOHN WEISS. Born in Boston, June 28, 1818; died there March 9, 1879. Graduated at Harvard and Divinity School, and was settled over Unitarian churches in Watertown and New Bedford, and preached for a time in the Hollis Street Church in Boston. He was a strong abolitionist, and a vigorous follower of the transcendental philosophy. He published "Life and Correspondence of Theodore Parker," 1864; "American Religion," 1871; "Immortal Life," 1880; and other works. The poems selected were printed in "The Radical." No collection of his poems has been published.

THOMAS WENTWORTH HIGGINSON. Born in Cambridge, December 22, 1823; in which city he now lives. Graduated at Harvard and Divinity School; settled over Unitarian church in Newburyport, and Free Church in Worcester. In 1858 withdrew from the ministry to devote himself to literature, and has since been an extensive contributor to periodicals, lectured widely, and published several volumes of fiction, essays, and history. He has been connected with all the later phases of the transcendental movement, and adheres to its cardinal beliefs. All the poems selected have been taken from "The Afternoon Landscape: Poems and Translations," 1888.

GEORGE SHEPARD BURLEIGH. Born in Plainfield, Conn., March 26, 1821, has spent most of his life in Little Compton, R. I., and now resides in Providence. He published "Anti-Slavery Hymns," 1842; "The Maniac, and Other Poems," 1849; and a translation of Victor Hugo's "La Légende des Siècles," 1867. He has been an editor, and a large contributor to the periodical press. He was zealous in the anti-slavery cause. The poems selected were contributed to "The Radical."

WILLIAM HENRY FURNESS. Born in Boston, April 20, 1802; died in Philadelphia, January 30, 1896. Graduated at Harvard and Divinity School, and was minister of Unitarian church in Philadelphia from 1825 to 1875. He published "Remarks on the Four Gospels," 1836; "Jesus and his Biographers," 1838; "The Veil Partly Lifted," 1864; "The Unconscious Truth of the Four Gospels," 1868, and other interpretations of the Gospels from the point of view of the idealistic philosophy. The poems selected are from his "Verses: Translations and Hymns," 1886.

SAMUEL JOHNSON. Born in Salem, Mass., October 10, 1822; died in North Andover, Mass., February 19, 1882. He graduated at Harvard and Divinity School, and was settled over the Free Church in Lynn from 1853 to 1870. Then he devoted himself to the writing of a series of books on "Oriental Religions," of which those on India, China, and Persia were published. His lectures, essays, and sermons were edited, in 1883, by Samuel Longfellow. The poems selected are from "Hymns of the Spirit," which he edited in 1864, in connection with Samuel Longfellow.

SAMUEL LONGFELLOW. Born in Portland, Me., June 18, 1819; died there, October 3, 1892. Graduated at Harvard and Divinity School, and was settled over Uni-

NOTES

tarian churches in Fall River, Mass.; Brooklyn, N. Y.; and Germantown, Pa. In connection with Samuel Johnson he edited "A Book of Hymns," 1846; and "The Hymns of the Spirit," 1864. The poems selected were first printed in the latter book. His biography has been written by Joseph May.

ELIZA SCUDDER. Born in Barnstable, Mass., November 14, 1821; died in Weston, Mass., September 27, 1896. Her "Hymns and Sonnets" were published in 1880; and this volume was republished by her cousin, Horace E. Scudder, 1896, who prefixed a brief memoir. Her "Hymns and Sonnets" was only a volume of a few pages when first published, and even in its enlarged form it is of only fifty pages. It contains some of the best hymns written in this country, however. Miss Scudder's life was spent in Barnstable, Salem, Weston, and Boston, and was one of few events. She was interested in the anti-slavery movement, was an earnest student, and was deeply concerned with the problems of the religious life. Her life was "one of much privation as regards health and fixed conditions, but she retained to the last an unappeasable hunger and thirst for intellectual food, and her companionship was a tonic, so invigorating was her spontaneous thought."

HELEN HUNT JACKSON. Born in Amherst, Mass., October 18, 1831; died in San Francisco, August 12, 1885. Her maiden name was Helen Maria Fiske. She married Captain Hunt, hence her name, Helen Hunt, "H. H." In 1875 she became Mrs. Jackson. She

323

published "Verses by H. H.," 1870; "Sonnets and Lyrics," 1876; "Mercy Philbrick's Choice," 1876; "Hetty's Strange History," 1877; "A Century of Dishonor," 1881; "Ramona," 1884. She is also thought to have written the "Saxe Holm Stories," from which the last two of the poems selected are taken.

EDWARD ROWLAND SILL. Born in Windsor, Conn., April 29, 1841; died in Cuyahoga Falls, O., February 27, 1887. Graduated at Yale, studied at Harvard Divinity School, but did not preach, and taught school in Ohio and California for several years. Was professor of the English language and literature in the University of California, 1874–1882. He published "Hermione, and Other Poems," 1866; and "The Hermitage, and Other Poems," 1867. After his death were published "The Venus of Milo, and Other Poems," 1888; and "Essays," 1900. In 1902 his complete poems were published.

JULIA WARD HOWE. Born in New York city, May 27, 1819, married Dr. Samuel G. Howe in 1843, and has since resided in Boston. Published "Passion Flowers," 1854; "Words for the Hour," 1856; "A Trip to Cuba," 1860; "Later Lyrics," 1866; "From the Oak to the Olive," 1868; "Modern Society," 1881; "Is Polite Society Polite? and Other Essays," 1895; "From Sunset Ridge," from which the poems selected have been taken, 1898; "Reminiscences," 1899. Mrs. Howe has closely identified herself with several phases of the later transcendentalism.

NOTES

EDNAH DOW CHENEY. Born in Boston, June 27, 1824, daughter of S. S. Littlehale. Married Seth Wells Cheney, the artist. Has taken an active part in promoting interests of women, has lectured much, and has been prominently connected with the Chestnut Street Club, Free Religious Association, and the Concord School of Philosophy. Mrs. Cheney lives in Jamaica Plain, a suburb of Boston. She has published "Faithful to the Light," 1870; "Sally Williams, the Mountain Girl," 1872; "Child of the Tide," 1874; "Life of Dr. Susan Dimock," 1875; "Gleanings in the Fields of Art," 1881; "Life, Letters, and Journals of Louisa M. Alcott," 1889; and "Stories of the Olden Time," 1890. The poems selected are taken from the appendix to her "Reminiscences," 1902.

JOHN BURROUGHS. Born in Roxbury, N. Y., April 3, 1837, and now lives at West Park on the Hudson River. He is well known for his books on outdoor subjects, from "Wake Robin," 1871, to "Signs and Seasons," 1886. He has been an ardent follower of Emerson and Whitman. He has published only a few poems. His "Waiting" was printed as a preface to the "Light of Day." The other poem appeared in his "Nature Poems," a volume of selections, 1902.

FRANKLIN BENJAMIN SANBORN. Born in Hampton Falls, N. H., December 15, 1831; and has lived in Concord, Mass., for many years. He was an intimate friend of Thoreau, Emerson, Alcott, and the other Concord literary people. Has been editor of "Boston Com-

monwealth," " Springfield Republican," and secretary of
Massachusetts State Board of Charities. He has pub-
lished biographies of Thoreau, John Brown, and Dr.
Samuel G. Howe. He has not collected his poems, but
they have appeared in Emerson's " Parnassus," " Con-
cord Lectures in Philosophy," and Stedman's " Ameri-
can Anthology." The poem on Emerson was read at
the Concord School of Philosophy, in 1882, and is the
concluding part of " The Poet's Countersign."

JOHN ALBEE. Born in Bellingham, Mass., April 3,
1833, and has resided for many years at New Castle,
N. H., but has recently removed to Chocorua, in the
same State. He has published " Literary Art," 1881 ;
" Poems," 1883 ; " Prose Idyls," 1892 ; " Reminiscences
of Emerson," 1901. He lectured at the Concord School
of Philosophy on poetry.

JOEL BENTON. Born in Amenia, N. Y., May 29, 1832 ;
and has lived in that place and in Poughkeepsie. He
has been a teacher, editor, and a frequent contributor
to the periodical press. He has published " Emerson as
a Poet," 1882 ; and "In the Poe Circle," 1899. His
poems have not been collected.

AUGUSTA COOPER BRISTOL. Born in Croydon, N. H.,
April 17, 1835, her father being Otis Cooper. Married
Louis Bristol in 1866. Has been lecturer and teacher,
and has resided for many years in Vineland, N. J. She
has published " Poems," 1868 ; "The Relation of the
Maternal Function to the Woman's Intellect," 1876 ;
"The Philosophy of Art," 1878 ; " The Present Phase

of Woman's Advancement," 1880 ; "Science and the Basis of Morality," 1880 ; and "The Web of Life" (poems), 1895. The poems selected were originally published in "The Radical."

ANNA CALLENDER BRACKETT. Born in Boston, May 21, 1836. Teacher in normal schools, and for twenty years principal of girls' private school in New York city. She was nine years principal of the St. Louis Normal School. Has written much on educational subjects, and has published "Education of American Girls," 1874; "Technique of Rest," 1892. Her poems have not been collected. Those selected first appeared in "The Radical," but the last one in "The Journal of Speculative Philosophy."

FRANCIS ELLINGWOOD ABBOT. Born in Boston, November 6, 1836. Graduated at Harvard, and was settled over Unitarian church in Dover, N. H. In 1870 began in Toledo, O., publication of "The Index," which was removed to Boston in 1873, and was continued till 1889. He was an active exponent of Free Religion until 1880, when he became a teacher. For several years he has been writing an extended work in philosophy. He has published "Scientific Theism," 1885 ; "The Way Out of Agnosticism," 1890. The poems selected were printed in "The Index" during the first year of its existence.

JOHN WHITE CHADWICK. Born in Marblehead, Mass., October 19, 1840. He has been minister of the Second Unitarian Society in Brooklyn, N. Y., since 1864. He has published biographies of Sallie Holley, Theodore Parker, and Dr. Channing, and many volumes of sermons, as well as several theological works. He has also published " A Book of Poems," 1876 ; " In Nazareth Town, and Other Poems," 1883 ; " A Legend of Good Poets," 1885 ; and " A Few Verses," 1900.

WILLIAM CHANNING GANNETT. Born in Boston, March 13, 1840. Has been settled over Unitarian churches in Milwaukee, Wis. ; Lexington, Mass. ; St. Paul, Minn.; Hinsdale, Ill. ; and Rochester, N. Y. He has published two volumes of " The Thought of God in Hymns and Poems," in connection with Frederick L. Hosmer, 1885, 1894.

FREDERICK LUCIAN HOSMER. Born in Framingham, Mass., October 16, 1840. Has been settled over Unitarian churches in Northboro, Mass. ; Quincy, Ill. ; Cleveland, O. ; St. Louis, Mo. ; and Berkeley, Cal. His poems have appeared in connection with those of William C. Gannett.

INDEX OF FIRST LINES

INDEX OF FIRST LINES

INDEX OF FIRST LINES

INDEX OF FIRST LINES

335

INDEX OF TITLES

INDEX OF TITLES

INDEX OF TITLES

INDEX OF TITLES

341